AF408260

Sally Alter http://sallyalter.com

Author of:
"How to Live with Bipolar"
"Bipolar 1 Disorder Rescue Plan: A Practical Guide for You and Your Family"
"A Practical Guide to Overcoming LONELINESS"
"We Never Did Mornings" (poetry)

Copyright © 2022 Sally Alter

LONELINESS

Contents

Introduction

I do hope you are not feeling lonely, but if you are this book is for you. I have written it with the intention of comforting and supporting people in their loneliness, so I hope it will be helpful to you.

As you probably know, there is a big difference between being alone and being lonely. One is a choice. The other is not. If you are alone by choice, that is fine, but if being alone makes you lonely then you need someone to be there for you. Hopefully, this book will be just the kind of book you are looking for.

LONELINESS encompasses one hundred and one questions and answers of all kinds of situations people find themselves in. I compiled this book from my answers on loneliness on Quora, the international question and answer website. I have written well over 4,000 answers on that website in the past two years, many solely on the subject of loneliness. I am also a registered Nurse and have taken care of many lonely people, especially seniors.

I have picked these questions and answers at random and hope they will be just what you are looking for. I have given much practical advice which I hope will be of use to you.

Many of the answers will include my experiences because I have had much loneliness in my life. My father died when I was ten and my mother followed him when I was fifteen, so I have been on my own a lot over the years. After my last husband died, I spent many lonely years trying to build up my life again. I have written all about these experiences in my answers and hope they will be able to help you.

Read this book and never feel lonely again.

Question 1

What is your best advice on living alone and overcoming the challenges that solitude and freedom can bring?

I am in my seventies and have lived on my own for the past twenty-two years since my husband died of suicide. Twenty-two years is a very long time to be alone. I have no family in this country, yet here I am, alive and well and really enjoying life as never before.

I am trying to think back now to see if I can answer your question truthfully.

The fact is that some people have no option but to live alone. Life is sometimes like that. Things happen and we are forced into a situation we don't necessarily want. Whether you go kicking and screaming, or relaxed and happy depends on a lot of different things.

In my case, I was very ill after my husband died and really could have done with somebody to help me. Many people asked me how I could live in my house after my husband had killed himself there? Well, that may sound like a reasonable question, but when the answer is I have no choice, it makes people realize that sometimes there is no choice in what we experience.

I have to admit to you the first few years were very hard. I suffered a great deal of loneliness and it was demoralizing. However, you eventually get used to your own company and can see many advantages to it.

I found a great therapist after my husband's death and am still with him today. He is responsible for keeping me alive, as staying alive was not something I wanted to do. As I say, I was very ill and there were many other reasons why I thought of ending my life which would not necessarily apply to other people.

However, I didn't succumb to that temptation and simply learned to adapt. If we don't adapt, we go into extinction like so many animals on the planet.

The way out of my dire situation was not through socializing and making new friends. It may be nice to do that, but it didn't work for me. I tried various churches and groups of people who were interested in the same things as me, but when you are alone everybody seems to be in couples and you are rarely invited to join them.

Learning to be alone and content is a process. It is really a process of learning to love oneself. This can take a very long time, or it may not happen at all. It all depends on how much effort you are willing to put into changing your lifestyle and way of thinking.

I changed my lifestyle by accepting that I was alone and not trying to do all the things that I used to take for granted when I was part of a couple. I did not yearn for somebody to talk to, nor did I want to go out and meet people. I simply realized that I could be happy on my own, and could even enjoy my own company.

As for loving myself, that did take a long time. Going from hate to love can seem insurmountable, but it certainly can be done. I am quite happy being me these days and am enjoying my solitude.

What eased my loneliness was adopting two cats early on as they were my lifeline. Sadly, both of these cats have since passed on, but I now have other cats to keep me company.

I also found that distractions are really important if you want to be happy with your own company. I have many hobbies and interests so can lose myself in those for many hours, sometimes forgetting to eat or drink anything.

My life is not the same as your life, though, so what you do will be different from what I do. Overall, I would say the thing that will save you is acceptance.

It is sometimes hard to accept things you don't want, but I can assure you that it can be done. Once you have accepted your situation, you will be free to love being by yourself.

Question 2

Do you sometimes feel that you will always be alone?

I can hear the fear in your question and can sense that you are not happy with your own company. That is very sad because sometimes our own company is all we have. People all around us may seem happy in their respective partnerships and it makes us feel left out. But all is not lost. We have a life, and must learn to live it.

If by chance you are left alone like me, it is not the end of the world, it is something to be cherished as not everybody gets the chance to understand themselves like we do.

Knowing yourself can be like going on a long journey. Some people yearn for it while others do not. But I have found that knowing my likes and dislikes has made me a happier person. I know just what I need out of life.

Which brings me to being alone with all its ramifications. It is true being alone can be hard, but it is only hard because we don't relish our own company. If I find myself alone, which I do more often than not, I accept that this is the plan that was laid down for me.

I have had a full life, so I do not yearn for things that cannot be any more because it only leads to disappointment. I shall probably be alone for the rest of my life. I am seventy-five in September and that is fine by me. I don't get out much, but I accept that nobody is likely to come knocking on my door if I don't make the effort to meet other people.

So, yes, I shall more than likely be on my own for a very long time, if I live long enough, but I am not scared by this. I know I could meet people if I wanted to, but at the moment I choose not to look for a companion.

18

If I was you and asking that question, I would want to know how I could be happy alone? It may just happen that someone does come knocking on your door. Until that day, learn to be happy in your own skin.

Question 3

Why do people use me then leave me? I feel really lonely, and don't know what I can do to help myself.

You are learning one of life's painful lessons, and what you are doing can often lead to loneliness. It is a sad thing but some people will use you if they possibly can. Simple as that. If you let them walk all over you, they will take all they can then discard you when they get bored with your company.

I have fallen for this situation countless times myself, and ended up licking my wounds when the friendship was over. I have allowed many people to take me for granted, then they have ended up expecting me to be there whenever they snapped their fingers. At first, you are doing them a favor, then before you know it, you are expected to be there whenever it is convenient for them. Favors can soon turn into obligations.

I can't count the number of rides I have given other people, the number of times I have got up in the middle of the night and helped people who were upset, or the number of meals I have served to people who never invited me back to their homes for dinner. In the past, I was a glutton for punishment, but have now learned my lesson.

The only way to tackle this problem is to work on your boundaries. Sometimes, we have leaky boundaries and do not realize where we end and the other person begins. If we allow it, that space between us can shrink. Then instead of keeping our own lives intact, we end up giving up what we want to do in order to please somebody else.

Another thing we tend to do when we have leaky boundaries is to overshare information. It is quite normal for people who have boundary issues to share anything and everything that pops into their head. Sometimes the other person just doesn't want to hear it, but other times it gives them ammunition to hurt us. It is very wise to measure your words and keep your distance with certain people. You will more than likely find that they never share anything with you.

If you don't want to be used anymore, you might need to think long and hard about what your boundaries really are. Only when you can decide what is good for you can you see your way clear to better relationships with other people.

Question 4

How do people manage to live alone for many years?

Living alone can be out of necessity as it is in my case. No matter how much I might want to live with somebody, if there is nobody there to live with, I will be on my own. It makes perfect sense.

People just don't seem to be able to understand that logic for some reason. I guess they have the choice which makes them think everybody else has that choice, but that is simply not true. More often than not, this applies to people who have no children and find themselves alone at the end of their lives. They cannot demand that somebody should come and live with them, can they?

The thing people don't realize is that living alone is a secret blessing. If you have never lived alone, you will not be privy to this secret, but, believe me, when you find yourself on your own, you will see what you have been missing.

There is a great deal to be said for doing what you please, when you please. You can come and go when you like, eat whatever takes your fancy, choose your own friends, and many other things besides. For example, I am sitting here in my nightdress at 11.30 in the morning, typing away to my heart's content. If I had somebody living with me, I would feel obliged to get dressed and make breakfast because that's how my life used to be.

Being alone can be fun. You will see. If you are given manure - relax. Out of manure comes the most beautiful roses.

Question 5

How can you live life on your own without needing anybody?

I have found that I can live on my own and be quite happy most of the time, but occasionally I need company and have a small number of friends I can spend time with. I have one friend who lives nearby and we have a lot of fun together. She is a "card" and makes me laugh all the time. I also have friends who I go to lunch with on occasion, and I look forward to those times when we can catch up with the gossip of the day. Those are the kind of friends you need when you are alone.

However, I have found it is hard to live alone when you are sick because you need other people for many reasons and they are often unavailable. When I had bursitis in my hip and could barely walk, I needed someone to take me to the doctor. And another time, I needed someone to take me for a minor procedure that required an anesthetic because it is hospital policy that you do not drive yourself home. And like many other people, I really hate to ask people to do me favors, so I pay them for their trouble.

If you are lucky enough to have a family living nearby, you will probably not have to struggle with these dilemmas. You will more than likely have somebody there for you all the time. I have no family where I live in Texas. My remaining sibling lives in Australia which is a long way to come to cat sit when I am taken into the hospital!

Of course, how much you need other people would depend to a great degree on your age. As we age, we tend to need more people to help us.

Other than that, I can recommend living alone because the freedom it brings is wonderful. I would not want to live with anybody else again.

Question 6

How can you combat feelings of loneliness after a divorce?

Personally, I found that when I was alone after my divorce, I couldn't fight the feelings of loneliness at all. They were just there, and I found no way to temper them. I was very lonely, and the walls felt as if they were caving in on me. I just wanted to scream, "Why me?" But, of course, why not me is the more suitable question. Also, I don't have any children so can't rely on them. Perhaps you are in the same boat as me.

When you find that you are totally alone with no one to call, it is nerve-wracking, and feels terrible. I used to say to myself: "I wish I had someone to call to tell them I have no one to call." How awful is that? Yet, I made a joke of it and usually had a little laugh at my own expense. I found that having a sense of humor helps the time pass more quickly, and it also keeps you feeling well.

But I was lonely, and used to count the number of people I knew on one hand. I decided they were all busy with their own lives and couldn't spare the time to talk to me. Saturdays were the worst. They came and went very slowly with me imagining that other people were enjoying being with their families and cooking steak on the grill like you see on TV. I went to church on Sundays, so at least I got out of the house and was able to find somebody to talk to.

I used to console myself by thinking that not every family is a happy one. For all the happy families there are, an equal number of miserable ones are out there. And I really believe that being in a terrible relationship is much worse than being alone. I know all about that, and feel quite relieved that I do not have to live that life again. My husband used to come round to see me after the divorce, but with no children to cement us together, we drifted apart.

24

Eventually, you do get used to being on your own after a divorce, and things sort themselves out without you trying. Even if you no longer have people to talk to, you can make a life for yourself by doing the things you like to do. Even if it is only surfing the web, or playing a game of Solitaire, keeping busy and distracted makes the time pass more quickly.

A lot of time has passed now, and I have people to talk to. But I can appreciate how terrible loneliness feels. I hope you will overcome these feelings soon.

Question 7

When should I accept that I will be on my own for the rest of my life?

Oh, that is really dismal, isn't it? I can imagine what state you are in to start thinking so negatively about your life. It sounds as if you have lost someone dear to you and you are now on your own, but not by choice.

I have to wonder how old you are because whatever your age I am sure you are younger than me. I am now seventy-four and expect to be alone for the rest of my life, but that is okay as I love my own company. If you are younger, you might be very surprised when your dream person comes into your life.

You can never really be sure about how long you will be alone. I am single and have no plans to marry, but if Mr. Right came into my life tomorrow, would I be single forever? Life might surprise me. Who knows?

If I were you, I would not waste a lot of time thinking of what might happen in the future as you can never really plan for the future no matter what it brings. You may think you have it all mapped out, only to find that something quite unexpected happens, then all your plans can change.

We can dwell in the past, but not be able to change it, or we can dwell in the future and not be able to change that either. It is always best to live in the present and let the future take care of itself.

Look on the bright side, concentrate on having some fun in your life, and you will probably meet someone nice when you least expect it.

Question 8

How can someone throw me away like trash after twenty-five years of marriage? I'm so alone, and don't want this life I'm living.

I am really sorry to read about your situation. It is very sad to think that someone can just leave you by yourself after twenty-five years of marriage, but that is what has happened. That is a fact.

I say that for a reason, so that you can acknowledge that this has actually happened to you. It is now in the past, and no matter how much you would like to change the past, you can never change anything that has already taken place. You are powerless to change the past or the future, but you can certainly change the present.

But first you have to get through the grief. Your hopes and dreams have come to nothing. Your marriage is over. There are no two ways about it, when you have lost something (even something that was not always perfect) you need to grieve over it.

So, before you can change your circumstances, you will have a period of quiet reflection where you can mull over your life and what has been lost. It will be a very sad time, I am sure, but so necessary before you can move on from here.

There is no saying how long you should grieve because everybody grieves differently. Some people seem to pick themselves up in no time, whereas others cannot shake their grief and it weighs them down.

In the end, you have to accept that your life with this partner is over, and you are left to choose to be happy in the future. This can mean all manner of things to different people, but I would just be open to whatever comes your way.

I believe that when something is lost it creates a vacuum and something even better will come along to fill it. I hope things will soon start to change for you.

Question 9

What is the difference between forced loneliness and self-imposed loneliness?

Your usage of the word lonely is misplaced as nobody chooses to be lonely. It cannot be self-imposed. You can choose to be alone, but that is quite different from being lonely. Loneliness is always a terrible thing to endure, and don't let anyone tell you differently. It is painful in a way that you can never understand unless you have experienced it for yourself.

I have spent many years feeling lonely at times and it is excruciatingly painful. I remember the feelings so well. It felt as if I was the only person left on this earth and there was nobody I could connect with.

If this is taken to extremes, and a person is alone for a very long time, they can easily start to think existential thoughts and wonder what life is all about. And indeed, many people go through the fear that they no longer exist. This is what some people call the dark night of the soul.

Many people are forced into loneliness because their partner dies, they lose a good friend, or something else of importance suddenly disappears from their life. This can also apply to pets. I know myself from losing three cats to various diseases, it is so painful it strikes you in the gut and makes it hard to breathe.

I personally prefer being alone, but it wasn't always that way. Once upon a time I lead a busy life and was never alone. That was fine with me at the time, but things have changed. Fortunately, after years of loneliness, I now feel fine.

Question 10

I feel so sad because nobody cares for me when I am sick. Do you think I will be alone forever? I am both bossy and picky. Is that why nobody likes me?

It is truly terrible when you feel lonely and nobody cares whether you live or die. I know how it feels to be sick and lonely. It is awful.

The phone never rings. Nobody comes round. You are just left there on your own feeling miserable.

The thing is, do you think that being bossy and picky is helping you in the friendship department? I would hazard a guess and say that the majority of people do not like being bossed around. And picky people can be very annoying.

Have you examined your life and asked yourself why you have these problems? After all, they are your problems, nobody else's. At least you are aware of them which is half way towards changing the patterns.

Are they problems you have had since childhood? Were you a bossy and picky child? If that is the case, you can see that this way of being in the world is very negative and detrimental to being happy. I think if you concentrated on these problems, and tried to make changes, you would be a much happier person.

I learned that needy people are boring, or downright scary. I was a needy person once who ran everybody out the back door. When you are needy, people feel obliged to help you. They do not do it out of love, they just feel that helping you is a duty they should perform. And nobody likes to get stuck in that position.

30

It is a good time for you to think about these things. Whether you call them flaws in your character is up to you. But it may behoove you to see what you can do to curb these tendencies. Try it.

Question 11

What are some things seniors can do for fun and not feel so lonely?

If you want to have fun and not feel so lonely, you must look for it outside of yourself. You need people. You sound as if you are a people person and that is good but you need to make an effort to get out there and do something enjoyable, then you won't be lonely.

We are very lucky to live in the 21st Century because there are simply so many things to do. I take it you have good health which is half the battle. When you have good health, you are free to do many things that people who are sick cannot contemplate doing.

Personally, I have too many things to do and not enough time to do them. It is an enviable position to be in because I am rarely bored or lonely. But you need to make a big effort to fill up your time and have fun.

I am sure you had fun when you were a kid. Think of all the things you did, and even all the things you wanted to do. Do them now while you are active. Seniors have many choices of things to do these days, so there is no excuse, unless you live way out in the country where you don't meet many people.

Surely, there are many things you can do in your town where you can meet other people? Here is a list of things off the top of my head:

- Swimming
- Join a gym
- Go to an evening class
- Take a coach trip with other seniors

- Join a walking group

- Join an art group

- Join a dance group

- Learn to play an instrument

- Take a course

- Play card games with others

- Join a church

- Join Toastmasters

- Volunteer

I could expand on this list if I wanted to because there are so many things you could do. Make a list of things you might like to try and start with those. Once you get out, you are sure to meet other people in your position so will not be lonely. You might even find that special person you want to be with. It can happen.

My brother is now ninety-one. When he was eighty-two, he met the love of his life at a photographic group. They got married and are very happy together. This could happen to you.

Question 12

Why do I feel so lonely when I have reached my goals and succeeded in the things I wanted to do?

First of all, congratulations on meeting your goals and succeeding in the things you wanted to do. How many people in the world can possibly say that? Most people don't have goals at all, and the ones who do are still striving for success. Not many people are in your position, I can assure you.

The problem most people have with goals is that they make them so big they are impossible to fulfill. When this happens, they can strive for years and never achieve anything. That is very disappointing. It is like New Year's resolutions. In January, people start out with a bang, but then give up in February as they have made their goal unattainable. Losing weight is a good example of this. So is cessation of smoking.

It doesn't seem as if you have this problem, though, which is very fortunate. For you, I would say make a difficult, time-consuming goal, something you can get your teeth into. At least you know you can be successful. With that knowledge, you are very likely to succeed.

Make a goal like writing a book which is all-consuming. It is very difficult to write a book, much more difficult than most people think. It can take many years of hard work. For you it would be an achievable goal, and one that would occupy your mind for a long period of time. That might be just the challenge you need.

I would go for something all-consuming like that. But maybe writing is not your thing. Even so, that could make the goal exciting because you have to learn something you may not think you have the aptitude for. The best thing to do is to plot your goal on the calendar and make smaller goals to work on every month. Do it in baby steps.

34

To be very honest, I am not sure what you mean by being lonely now that you have reached your goals because the two do not seem to go together. Loneliness is a state of mind caused by a lack of social relationships. Whereas, meeting a goal is a personal challenge, often done alone. Perhaps you want to find a goal that can be shared with other people.

You will have to think long and hard about this. First, you will need to find a group of people who are doing things that interest you, then you can join them.

Question 13

What advice can you give to someone who is currently single and lonely?

I have to admit it is difficult to be single and lonely. Some people may even envy your situation because, believe it or not, many people are lonely even if they are in a relationship and have many friends. We just do not realize this when we are single. We think everybody else is happy and getting on with their lives.

It is difficult to give advice because many times it seems impossible to change your situation. Some people go to church and meet people. Others join clubs and share interests with people in their area. But if you do not want to do something like this, you will be by yourself and lonely.

There is nothing wrong with feeling like that. When you are lonely it seems as if nothing can ever make you feel happy again. It may be true that at the present time you are single and lonely, but as often happens, you meet someone and forget all the lonely times you had before. It may seem out of the question right now, but you would be surprised how many people actually do meet someone when they least expect it. Many people do online-dating these days. Apparently, a third of all marriages are between people who met online. Times are changing.

In the meantime, while you are waiting for this special person to come into your life, why not take the opportunity to get to know yourself. Do things that please you. Take up a new hobby, learn a language, do things that take you out of yourself. You might find that when you are absorbed with interests or hobbies, the time passes very quickly and you forget where you are.

I have many creative interests that take me out of myself. Creativity is a right brain activity and time passes without you realizing it. I find many hours can go by without me being aware of them.

If you find something totally absorbing like artwork or music, you will wonder why you were ever lonely because time will pass quickly. And if you never meet that perfect companion, you will eventually get used to your own company.

Question 14

Sometimes I feel like crying because nothing good is happening in my life. I have not achieved my dream, don't have friends, and have lost interest in everything. How do I cope with this?

It sounds to me as if you are depressed. You have some of the symptoms of depression, namely a sense of failure, a fear that nothing good will happen in your life, and a lack of motivation to make something happen. And when you mention crying, it is something that happens a lot with depression. People cry for no conceivable reason. Tears just come.

I would say you would do well to see your doctor so that you can start on an appropriate treatment. Anti-depressants take about two to three weeks to work, so you would be wise to start as early as possible if you think you are depressed. Go to see your doctor and talk it over with him. He would be better able to diagnose depression than me and would be able to help you cope with it.

You say you have not achieved your dream. What was your dream? Maybe it was unrealistic in the first place. Dreams can cost a lot of money, or they can depend on luck. Life rarely works out the way we want it to. It is amazing you can plan all you like, then something quite unexpected comes up and your life changes. Sometimes for the worse, but maybe for the better.

I have not achieved my dream of living in France, mostly due to illness. Perhaps this has happened to you. We just cannot plan these things. Now I think I have missed the boat and will never live in France because I am in my seventies. Fortunately, I have achieved success in other ways, and so can you.

Have you tried making a vision board? Many people do that and swear it works. A vision board is said to work because you can see your dream right there in front of you every day. Buy a piece of foam board, gather together a pile of colorful magazines, (you can get these in most used clothing stores), then cut out pictures of things you would like to have in your life. You may find pictures of people you would like to meet, houses you would like to live in, or even vacations you would like to go on. It is your dream and your vision board, so you can do what appeals to you. When it is ready, hang it in a place where you can see it every day and your dreams may come true.

Question 15

I don't have any family or friends and feel so alone. I don't make friends well, either. What can I do to improve my situation?

I am sorry you feel alone, but can see why. You miss having people in your life. However, it is a fact that you have no family or friends and, as I am sure you will agree, it is very hard to change that situation.

You ask what you can do to improve your lot, and I believe I might have the answer. It may not be a palatable answer because it is spiritual by nature, but it may keep you from feeling lonely. It seems to me that you are meant to be alone because you are learning one of life's essential spiritual lessons. That is the law of non-attachment.

Most people suffer from attachment. They are attached to their family, their friends, their pets, their jobs, even their cars. In fact, everybody seems to be attached to something. But when it comes to attachment, the price is pain.

The moment that person, pet, job or anything else disappears from their lives, the pain starts. And it can be excruciating. How many people are suffering from divorce, or the loss of a job? And how many people are suffering from the loss of someone dear to them? The best and the most uncomplicated way of living is to be detached from everything.

Non-attachment is a real problem for the majority of people. They don't know how to escape from the pain. But if you want to be happy and live a pain-free life, then learn the lesson of non-attachment.

If you think about it, you are already half way there because you are not attached to anybody. If you think about it like that, you will see that you are lucky. You are already living the spiritual truth of non-attachment. If you still feel pain, you still have some learning to do.

If you are able to detach from the material world you will find that you can live practically pain- free. It gives you a wonderful sense of freedom. I learned this truth some time ago, and feel more at peace when I can detach from everything. I can't say I am always successful, though, as I am only human like you.

Question 16

How can I be happy alone?

That is an interesting question as it supposes that everybody else manages to be happy when they are alone, but you cannot. There is a sense of failure there. Something to be ashamed of. Yet, this is false as many people feel just like you and would love to know how to be happy when they are on their own.

Obviously, not everybody is happy with their own company, and many people just can't seem to find peace in their solitude. Some people look upon it as a curse - a punishment for crimes unknown. And loneliness can seem very punitive at times. Yes, it can be scary to find yourself alone in the world, but you can always reach out to others sometimes. We are not meant to be lone wolves.

Of course, without knowing your circumstances I cannot give you a good answer as I don't know how old you are, if living alone is new to you, or if you have tried being happy and failed.

Whatever your story, one thing you can be sure of is that you need to change your way of thinking. If you continue to think of being alone as a bad thing. you will always have trouble finding ways to make yourself happy. Being alone can be a very good thing if you think of it positively.

The best thing you can do I to think about the things you can do to pass the time. Time can drag on when you are on your own and have nothing to do. I know many people leave jobs then find that they can't fill their days with anything to interest them. So many hours are passed at work that it is very hard to fill them if you are bored. If you are fit enough to work, even part time, that can be very good for you. It is nice to feel useful and to have a social life. It gives you a lot of confidence. Or try volunteering, or meeting people for lunch. If you really have nobody, try making friends online.

42

Turn your circumstances around and see the positive side of things. If you can't change your situation, the only option left to you is to adapt. Humans are very adaptable. We can adapt to most things if we put our mind to it.

Question 17

I have two daughters and have given them everything. Now they have both moved away and cut me out of their lives. What should I do?

Right at the start, I have to be honest and tell you that I do not have any children so cannot advise you directly from experience. I always wanted a family, but none ever came, so I am having to make the best of a life without children and grandchildren.

I can see that you loved your daughters, and probably did your best for them, but they don't bring you joy because they have cut ties with you. This is very sad and upsetting, and I am sorry it has happened to you.

You don't give me any details about your daughters or the situation, so I can only guess. I wonder if they have children and you are missing your grandchildren. That would be very difficult for you, I am sure.

Unfortunately, I cannot wave a magic wand and make everything right between you and your daughters. Perhaps you have tried everything already and nothing good has come of it. Of course, in these days of social media it is much easier to keep in touch with family. People are able to send photos and videos across the miles. Perhaps you have tried this and it has failed. I don't know. But it certainly seems as if the situation is one that is not easy to change.

One thing I do know, though, is situations do change over time. Things may seem static at the moment, but that is not to say your daughters will be estranged from you forever. Something might happen to bring them back into your life one day. In the meantime, I would try to accept the situation for what it is. It is sad, I know, but that is how things turn out sometimes. If you have done all you can to reach out to them, then all you can do now is wait and see what happens.

I do hope you will hear from them again. And if you have grandchildren, I hope you will be able to be part of their lives. Good luck to you.

Question 18

Is it easier for women to live alone?

Living alone has its pluses and minuses for a woman or a man. Like everything else in life, there are two sides to every coin. One is bleak, the other hopeful. It is no different with living alone.

The difference may be that women living alone are generally more capable because they are able to cook and keep house. They also seem more adaptable to being alone than men. Men may also be able to look after themselves, but don't like living alone. It is quite common for them to look for a partner even shortly after being widowed.

But I am generalizing here. You can't lump people together and say they are all the same. People are different. They have different tastes, talents, wishes and pet peeves. Some women are great housekeepers and don't mind being alone, while others have never cooked a meal in their life.

The same goes for men. Some men like living alone and wouldn't have it any other way. Whereas, other men are never happy with their own company, and want someone there to look after them.

I have lived on my own for many years and have not only survived, but thrived. I would never go back to living with anybody else again. I might like to have a relationship with somebody, but I would not want to share a house with them. I much prefer my own company.

Whether it is easy or not depends on the person. Some people do not adjust to life alone and suffer dreadful loneliness. I know about loneliness because I spent many years feeling lonely myself. But now that I have adjusted and accepted my single status, everything is fine.

Here are some of the minuses I have found when living on my own:

- Nobody there to unscrew jars!

- Nobody to discuss the everyday things that happen.

- Nobody to prepare a meal for.

- Nobody to walk hand in hand with around the park.

- Nobody to help make major decisions.

- Nobody to help pay the household bills.

- Nobody to go out to eat with at a restaurant.

- Nobody to fix things around the house.

- Nobody to deal with cantankerous plumbers, a/c techs, computer techs, electricians, gardeners, housekeepers and everything in between.

- But living alone can be fun, too:

- Nobody to tell you when to go to bed.

- Nobody to tell you when to get up.

- Nobody to tell you when to cook dinner.

- Nobody to shout at you when things go wrong.

- Nobody to argue over the thermostat.

- Nobody to argue over the remote.

- Nobody to tell you where you can go.

- Nobody to tell you when to come back.

- Nobody to interrupt you when you are busy.

- Nobody to complain when you want to be quiet.

So, you can see that life is just one big adjustment. Whether you are male or female, the only thing for it is to adjust to things the way they are.

Question 19

What should I do when I feel alone? I live far away from my family and there is no-one to share my feelings with. I have made some friends but they're not interested in my feelings.

You are like me. You are a feeling type of person; you mentioned feelings three times in your question. The first thing to do is to sort out your feelings from the facts.

You can't feel alone, but you can feel lonely. Being alone is just a fact. Like I have dark hair and blue eyes. These are facts and being alone is another fact. Being lonely is a feeling.

However, I certainly see your dilemma as you are stuck with your feelings and nobody wants to hear about them. The world is full of thinkers. Thinkers think and rarely feel, or at least they rarely share their feelings with other people. I know what you mean because I tend to be surrounded by thinkers who don't share their feelings, as well. I have made many friends in the past who are only interested in my thoughts and never share their feelings with me.

I used to try to share my feelings with all these thinkers, but when I saw it was a waste of time, I stopped and kept my feelings to myself. People generally are not interested in other people's feelings. They often find them embarrassing or overwhelming. And some people think about how they are feeling when you mention your feelings, and they are often shocked at how bad they feel themselves.

The thing to do is to share your feelings with something safe like a journal. Journals are hardy souls. They do not care how much you share your feelings with them because they never get upset. A journal is a fine way to cope with your feelings because you can pour your heart out and it doesn't matter. Your journal will always listen to you no matter how bad you feel.

Another thing that is great for sharing your feelings with is a pet. Pets love you, come rain or shine, and just love to listen to all your secrets. See if you can find a pet who you can share your feelings with.

I have a cat who knows how I feel about everything because I take her into my confidence. She is a great secret-keeper too. We have our little secrets together.

So, my advice to you is to stop trying to share your feelings with all these thinkers and find another way to share how you feel. Good luck.

Question 20

I've always been alone with no friends since I was a child. Why does it hurt to be alone?

I can see why it hurts you to be alone, and would think you have been hurting for a very long time as you say you have had no friends since you were a child. I would love to know if you were an only child as this can be one reason why people do not make friends when they are children or when they are older.

Only children don't seem to mix well at school, and don't do well in groups or teams. Team sports are often a big problem for people who never had anybody to play with when they were young. This may apply to you, I don't know. It certainly applied to me. Even today, I do not do well in groups or teams of any kind.

But I do not mind spending time alone in my house. I have plenty of things to entertain me, and you could find things to do, too. Perhaps you are a decorator and could make your house more comfortable. Maybe you like cooking or flower arranging. Perhaps you have a garden you could potter about in. All these things are creative, and I find creativity is very satisfying, especially when you are on your own. If you don't like doing any of these things there is always the internet to entertain you. You can spend many happy hours online, playing games, learning a language or generally broadening your knowledge.

One thing I do know is that it is often difficult to be seen alone in public. I tell myself that other people are not looking at me, and don't care about me, but when I eat alone in a restaurant, I do feel self-conscious and wish I had somebody to talk to. However, as I like to eat, I do occasionally eat out on my own.

I wonder how you feel when you are alone in public. Do you feel self-conscious when you are seen outside the house on your own? It is a vastly different situation than being at home on your own, and some people avoid being out in public on their own at all costs.

I think the reason it is difficult to be seen alone when in public is because people think you are alone because you have nobody to be with. This is often true, of course, and it is embarrassing. To have nobody to be with can be a very sad situation to find yourself in. It can even feel shameful.

If you want to make friends with other people, you may need to push yourself out of your comfort zone. Go to a church or a club and see if you can join in and feel part of things. You would get the opportunity to brush up on your social skills then.

Question 21

How do you become immune to loneliness?

The only way to become totally immune to loneliness is to become a robot. That is not helpful, I know, but I want to make a point that if we are human, we are likely to be lonely at some point in our lives. As many people say, you can be lonely in a crowd. And this is true of some people. Many people say they are lonely in their marriage and that is very sad indeed.

Many people are lonely. It is not unusual. You certainly can't become immune to it, though, because loneliness is not a disease. You can't get a shot in the arm to prevent loneliness. Being lonely is a situation you find yourself in, and many people find it uncomfortable.

I have had many lonely years in my life, but I got through it, and so will you. Loneliness is painful, there is no doubt about that, but if you just accept that it is knocking on your door once again, you will be able to cope with it.

I am not saying you will be able to overcome it, as loneliness has a bad habit of looking us up again from time to time, but I am saying that you can work your way through it.

I think staying busy can help. If you have some purpose in your life, it will make a huge difference. It is not good to live a life without a purpose anyway. We all need to feel that we have a reason for being here on this earth, so you need to find out what you are good at and do that.

I would love to tell you that you will not be lonely as time goes by because, even when you least expect it, loneliness can creep in. Just ride the waves of loneliness and know that you can get through it in time.

Question 22

Do you think loneliness is a phenomenon of depression?

This is an interesting question because loneliness is not strictly a symptom of depression. However, many people who are depressed are lonely because they isolate themselves and never see or hear from anybody. To make matters worse, they sometimes stop using social media, don't answer the phone, and don't even answer the door, so people stop trying to communicate with them. This depressive state can indeed lead to loneliness.

Older people, living on their own, are often depressed. They may not have much contact with people in their normal daily lives, so when they are depressed, there is nobody to check on them and see if they are safe. This can be a dangerous situation as suicide is always a risk with depression.

When a person is depressed, they have many other symptoms due to the illness. Most lose all motivation to do anything, so days can pass by without them taking care of themselves. It is quite common to stop eating when depressed, and many people have no energy to pay attention to their hygiene. They feel sad and hopeless and usually have a problem with sleep.

Naturally, these symptoms make a person more depressed, and if they have no support, they will be cut off from society altogether. Even a person who is not depressed might be lonely at times. But a person who is depressed will be affected more than others.

Question 23

What is too much solitude? What are the signs?

Some people have no idea what solitude means. Just being alone for a couple of hours may be solitude for some, but I am sure that is not what you asking here.

Just imagine you are sitting in a chair, no bound to a chair, and I am forcing food down your throat. You have already eaten your meal, but I am forcing you to eat another meal that you do not want.

How do you feel? Really uncomfortable, no doubt about it.

Nobody is forcing solitude on you, and when you start to feel uncomfortable with being on your own you will know for sure that you have had enough.

Being by yourself is great, but there comes a time when you just want to throw up your hands and say, "Enough already." That is when you know you want to be around people again.

It is nice to have friends to be with, but even if you don't have friends, you can be around other people in church, at the supermarket or at the doctor's office. This may not be ideal, but I find that I can talk to people in the line at the store with no problem at all. If you find that you are feeling uncomfortable with too much solitude, I do hope you will search out some people to spend time with.

Question 24

Does traveling solo get lonely or scary, or does a person get used to it?

I have intentionally traveled alone a couple of times and have also traveled alone with the intention of meeting people at my destination. The times I have met people have been fun because I had something to look forward to, and meeting up with people I hadn't seen for a long time was good. But traveling alone in a party of holiday makers spelled doom and gloom for me.

At one time, I went on a coach trip to Costa Rica on my own. I have no idea why I did this except to say I wanted to see Costa Rica and that was the only way I was going to be able to do it.

That holiday was the holiday from hell.

I have bipolar disorder and learned my lesson over that period of nine days that I am not meant to be on my own for long trips. If anything could go wrong, it did, and I was left in tears much of the time. I had panic attacks every day and was a complete mess. I felt very vulnerable and lonely and just wanted to go home.

The people in the coach party must have thought I was odd because they avoided me like the plague. I can't blame them because my behavior was very strange. I became so ill on that holiday that it should have ended in a hospital visit in a foreign country.

So, for me, I can honestly say that I was lonely and scared. Whether I could have got used to it is another matter. I think I probably would have got used to it if I had been well, but not when I was going through such turbulent times with my illness. Also, traveling, especially to other time zones, plays havoc with bipolar disorder.

Of course, I don't know your situation so can't comment on it. Hopefully, you are healthier than I was at that time and would enjoy your trips enormously. You would have to decide if you wanted to be a member of a group, like a coach party, even though you were alone. Some people fare really well, chat to their fellow travelers and have fun sight-seeing and absorbing the culture. They often do a lot of research of the area before leaving home and this seems to keep people busy during the trip. Personally, I don't do any research because I like the element of surprise, but have missed things in the past that I might otherwise have seen.

There was one woman on my coach trip who had a wonderful time. You could tell. She was quite young, maybe thirty, and had a very friendly disposition. She casually chatted to everybody but also seemed perfectly happy to spend time on her own. I must say, I rather envied her as I was unable to blend in like that. I sometimes wonder if I could have had more fun on that coach trip now that I am well.

Question 25

What did you do when you realized you will be alone for the rest of your life?

I'll tell you what you do, you realize that being alone does not necessarily mean that you will be lonely. Being alone is fine, but being lonely is terrible. I have been through both scenarios and have survived to tell the tale.

When I was first alone, many years ago, I was very lonely. Every day was a nightmare because I had nobody to talk to. I noticed sharing things like passing the time of day with someone became important to me. Just commenting on mundane things and being heard was the stuff of life. I could comment on a new bird at the bird feeder and there was nobody there to say, "Oh, yes, let's look him up in the bird book."

I also noticed that sharing decisions was very important. It soon becomes apparent that there are many decisions to be made in any partnership, and there is nobody there to share disasters when they occur.

When the a/c breaks down in the middle of the summer there is nobody there to share the decision of which company is more reliable to fix the a/c system. You find you have to try them all, and when you are a single woman, it soon becomes apparent that there are many rogues out there who profess to be something they are not.

When you are young and single these things do not matter because people will go out of their way to be helpful, but as you age so does the available help. It becomes old very quickly.

So, when you are old and single you had better be prepared to feel lonely much of the time. At least at first. But as human beings, we eventually get used to situations. People can endure the worst of situations and still live quite peacefully.

Over time, sometimes a very long time, your particular situation begins to take on a new light. Rather than feeling the sting of loneliness, you find that you are beginning to enjoy your own company. It can be quite a surprise. How could you have ever imagined you would prefer being alone? Yet, that is what has happened to me and I daresay it happened to many other lonely, single people.

Over time, I have adapted to being alone and plan on being alone for the rest of my life. I look back with amusement sometimes because I was a social butterfly when I was young, always surrounded by company, always craving more. Now, I no longer crave company. In fact, I generally shy away from it.

I notice these days that I am quite content with my hobbies and my cat, and when my day is interrupted by people, I get bored almost immediately and just want to be alone again.

My friends are few and far between. But I don't mind. If I have a couple of people to talk to every now and then, it is enough for me. I don't need to be texting and talking on the phone for hours like some people do.

My quiet life is just that. Quiet. I get up when I have had enough sleep. I jump in my car and go for a drive if the mood takes me, and there is nobody there to complain.

I was married to a big-time complainer for many years. I felt chained like a dog in the yard. My chain wasn't long enough to stay out of the sun, and my bowl of water was always out of reach.

Now, I have dropped that chain for good, and I can please myself whenever I choose.

Question 26

I had a guideline for how I wanted to live my life, but somewhere along the way, I gave in for fear of not being accepted. What is it like to lose yourself?

This is a very complex situation and one I am not sure I understand without speaking to you in person. I do know, though, that many people are afraid of not being accepted and try to change who they are in the process.

When you say you had a guideline, it would seem that you were trying to live by a script instead of just accepting who you were and being spontaneous. Surely, that is a very unnatural way to live and can only end in disaster?

Life is not predictable. Life can be tumultuous and difficult to understand. If you were living by a script, you would be certain to go off course whenever something unexpected happened.

Many people make plans for the future. It is not unusual. But what is unusual is that the plans come to fruition. People die young, lose their jobs, get sick. All manner of things happen that can change their plans completely. And as for saving for the future, you never know what might happen in the meantime as so many people have found out. Even companies providing pension schemes to employees is a thing of the past now leaving people with only social security to rely on in their old age.

I accept that many people do have more or less predictable lives. They certainly seem to be living by a script. They grow up, get married, have children, work and die. It is pretty much predictable, and I think it would be very boring.

I wonder why you feel fear of acceptance, but do know that this is a very common fear. Many people have so much fear of not fitting in that they never venture out to meet people. The only way I know to combat that fear is to muster your courage and go out to meet people if that is what you want to do.

Whether you can lose yourself because you have changed your script is another thing entirely. I don't think you can ever lose the real you. If you don't like yourself, it is up to you to change what you are doing and how you are thinking.

Question 27

When someone is grieving is it appropriate to help them take their mind off of things, or would they rather be left alone?

Grieving is a journey that must be taken alone.

That does not mean there is no life on the road to their destination. It just means the journey must be a solo one in order to get to the other side. This can be a very lonely journey indeed.

Being alone or being with somebody is irrelevant because the journey is private. It may be good to distract the person with a meal or a visit on occasion because the road is an uphill climb and many need to find their breath along the way.

Disbelief

The first part of the journey cannot be taken with anybody at all because the person is literally 'in shock' and cannot be rescued or helped in any way. The life blood drains out of them as they rock back and forth, or even try to stand.

Nobody can give them a transfusion to get them to their destination. They must wait patiently for the blood to fill the vessels again.

Fury

The next part of the journey can last for months, even years. Fury is all consuming and horrible. The body is tense and can remain so for a very long time. The mind is swirling in chaos. There is no room in that person's life for other people to enter.

The fury is often misdirected at whomever is seen as complicit in their loved one's death. It is directed at doctors, relatives, ministers, and even oneself. Everybody bears the brunt of the grieving person's fury. The fury at God is often the hardest part of all because of the guilt that goes with it. But even this shall pass.

Negotiating

The next part of the journey is less cluttered with rocks. It is still difficult for the person to walk as it is painful on that part of the road. Negotiating is fruitless. It doesn't work for anyone. The person is dead, there is no point negotiating with God or anybody else to change what is now the truth.

But other people can help on this part of the road as it is smoother and the person is more amenable to conversation. Changing the course of the journey is not possible, though, as it is already underway.

Sadness

Sadness is the loneliest part of the journey and, if left unchecked, can go on for months or even years. It is the part of the road called depression and it is full of potholes. The person finds they can walk for a short time on smooth ground then suddenly they trip up and fall into a pot hole. It is black and full of mud. The mud is thick and there is no way they can climb out of the pothole. Nobody can help them on this part of the journey no matter how hard they try.

All energy is gone and the crying begins. When the crying begins it never stops. It is a plea for release, but release is slow to come. The body is weak and the mind is blank. Thoughts are not constructive and there's no working things out.

Destination

Finally, the person will come to the end of the road. This is the part of the journey where the sun comes out from behind a cloud and the air is fresh to breathe. Others are welcomed in at the destination.

Life can begin again.

The awful thing is that all the tracks on the road can sometimes converge making life even more confusing than it was. There are steep mountains, rocks and pot holes and they are mired in dread. The journey is unpredictable, going round in circles, and the journey must be undertaken again and again.

You may find it very difficult to reach your destination, and this is where professional, medical advice is advised.

Many people have overlapping symptoms that make it very difficult to get to their destination. They are furious one minute, then sad the next. They think they have got over the disbelief, but it suddenly comes back to haunt them. The only thing that can be done is to accept what is happening as acceptance is key to every problem.

(Modified from the work by Elizabeth Kubler-Ross "On Death and Dying.")

Question 28

What is the difference between enforced isolation and time spent in solitude?

There is a vast difference between enforced isolation and solitude because one is a choice and the other is not.

A person who is forced to live in isolation could be a person who is in solitary confinement in prison and is only let out of their cell for one hour a day. There is nobody to talk to because the guards come, often without speaking, and just shove food through a hole in the bars. You may get letters from home if you are lucky. You don't have any further means of communication because you do not have a telephone or a computer. And, because of this you lose touch with the world outside of your cell.

That is cause for alarm, and often sends a person into a deep depression. Some people even have psychotic episodes when they are in solitary confinement. Of course, it is meant to be a punishment so there is no choosing your fate.

Now, take the situation of a person who chooses to live in solitude. They would naturally be alone if they had no visitors and didn't go out. However, most people who live alone these days do have a means of communication. They can telephone people when they like, watch TV or spend time on the computer.

The people who have been forgotten are those who do not chose to live in solitude. This describes many thousands of people in this country. They do not have friends or relatives, they just exist in dire circumstances, coping with health problems and loneliness. Finances can be tight and some do not even have enough money to buy food. Without communication by phone, television or computer it can be a lonely life.

I often think of what it was like to be a woman in the pioneer days in America. They waited to see their husbands from sun up to sun down as they were out on the ranch. There was little means of communication with the outside world. Spending time baking, cooking, cleaning, and looking after the children must have been very lonely indeed.

They certainly didn't have all the luxuries we take for granted these days, but I wonder if they had books, apart from the bible, to bring them in contact with the outside world?

You can see that communication with other people is very important. It reminds us that we are human.

Question 29

How does one cope with the fact that they'll be alone forever and not accomplish anything in life?

To be alone should not be the end of your dreams. It is not about shutting off all sense of purpose, shriveling away, and never gaining ground. You are above all that. There should not be a sense of the inevitable. You are not powerless. You need to realize that you are the most powerful person in the world when it comes to shaping your own future.

Your present experience may be bad, your thoughts may be bleak, but the reality is that you can change those thoughts, and the future, if you only put your mind to it. There is nothing written that says you will be alone forever. And nothing further from the truth that you can't accomplish anything in life.

But if you do find yourself alone, accepting one's aloneness is key.

We are all alone, even in the midst of a crowd. We have to take responsibility for changing our lives. You cannot sit back and expect things to change. You must make change happen in order to grow.

I am speaking from experience here as I thought my life would be wasted and I would never fulfill a purpose. It took me a very long time to make changes in my life, but now that I have, I feel so much happier. By writing books, I feel I have a purpose. I am communicating with other people and, hopefully, making their lives more meaningful.

Broaden your interests and your experiences. Do the things you never had time for before. Strive to learn something new every day.

Question 30

How do you get over a bad marriage and be happy alone late in life?

I fall right into your category as an older person whose bad marriage came to an end, so can answer your question from a personal point of view. Having written so many times about this subject, I haven't got much to add except to say that I was lonelier in my marriage than I am today.

People seem to worry about being alone an awful lot, but there really is nothing to fear. Once you have got over the fact that there is nobody there at the dinner table to talk to and nobody to snuggle up to in bed, loneliness does not play a part. You may even be better off on your own, and I know I am not the only person out there who feels this keenly.

The more I think of it now, the more I realize how lucky I am to be free of the painful loneliness I felt in the midst of my marriage.

Things were not bad at all when we lived in England as I had a nursing job to go to, friends around me, and more than enough to occupy my time. It was one thing to say goodbye in the morning, to spend the day surrounded by people, then to come home to a full house in my bed and breakfast every night. No chance of loneliness then. I was caught up in a social whirl and never imagining what lay ahead.

My husband was very amenable to me in those days, as he was to all our guests. He was a buzz of life - cooking, cleaning and all the things a full-time bed and breakfast owner does when his wife is at work.

But this is not a true situation. It is just a farce - nothing to do with two people, who as it turned out, did not know each other at all.

Then when we moved to the U.S. and toured the country in a motorhome, things took a turn for the worst as we were too close for comfort. It became a situation of having someone else say your words, think your thoughts and control the rest of your life. I lost who I was in his desires, wishes and demands until I couldn't recognize myself. That is what loneliness was made of in my case.

If you have escaped a marital situation like mine and many thousands of others, you will find that being alone is far preferable. Good luck to you.

Question 31

My sister has lived alone for three years since her husband died. She says she is lonely and wants to live with me. I am happy with my own company and don't want to share my house with anyone. What should I say to her?

Well, that is a very honest question., one you have obviously thought about a great deal. It would seem to me you have already decided you don't want your sister to live with you because you state that quite clearly.

It seems to be a problem that you don't want to confront, so have left it on the back burner hoping that she will change her mind. But, as you say, she has been alone for a few years since her husband died and she is lonely. It seems she thinks she can live with you and all will be well.

However, you have been perfectly happy with your own company and don't yearn for somebody to talk to. It often takes people quite a while to get to that stage in life.

I wonder how you get on with your sister, and if you have any clashes of opinions. Seeing as you were probably brought up by the same set of parents, it is likely that you have the same, or similar beliefs about the world. This would be an important point to consider if you are thinking you might have to let her move in.

People generally form their belief systems from their parents, and not many people question these beliefs as they grow older. But some people do think about their beliefs and then they clash with their family's opinions about the world. There could be differences of opinion about religion, politics, money, family, even staying up late with the TV on too loud. If this is the case, then you might have a very contentious relationship.

It all boils down to how your sister's move would affect your daily life. Personally, I am just like you and happy with my own company. I could not see my way clear to living with anyone, not even a relative. Or perhaps, especially a relative!

I would think about this very carefully. She may be lonely but that is not necessarily a good reason for moving in with somebody. There are so many other things to consider. Do you have enough room in your house, for example? Would she want to join you for every meal? Would she want to share the housework and shopping? Would she want to share the bills? There are so many considerations when you share your living space with another person.

If it was me, I would realize that this is it is a life-changing situation. You may not feel like saying no to her now, but if you really don't want her to move in, it will save you a lot of aggravation in the future. For the time being, I would put her off by saying you love her but don't think you want to share your home with anyone. It will hurt, no matter what you say or how you say it, but it might hurt less than having her around if that is something you do not want.

Question 32

I am very lonely, but not the type of person to mix well with others. I have been invited to a wedding and feel I should go, but I am reluctant to meet a lot of other people. What should i do?

I can see your dilemma, but the answer depends on a lot of things. You don't say how close you are to the bride or groom. Or perhaps you are close to their immediate family. You don't say if you usually go to this type of occasion even though you feel scared about going.

It would seem to me that you have quite a few choices and it would do well to consider them one by one. For a start you could refuse to go at all. You could come up with some excuse like you are sick. I know it is a little lie, but it may save you a lot of anxiety in the long run.

You could also go and not stay too long. Set a time limit and stick to it. Maybe you could to stay for an hour and a half, or if that is too long, half an hour. You could then make your excuses and leave. I don't like going to big gatherings either, and usually stay for an hour and a half. I find half the time I am not missed by anyone when I leave.

The other suggestion is you can go and make up your mind to enjoy yourself. It would help with your loneliness, after all. You might find someone interesting to talk to and even enjoy the food! I always hover near the banquet at big occasions like weddings and have a pretty good time!

Whatever you decide to do, make sure you send a gift for the bride and groom. If the gift comes with an excuse not to come to the wedding, at least you will show that you haven't forgotten them.

With big gatherings like this, I usually find that I get lost in the crowd and can sneak away when it suits me. I hope you will make the right decision.

Question 33

What advice really works for lonely people?

How I would love to wave a magic wand and make loneliness go away forever. I have experienced many years of loneliness myself and know how soul-destroying it is. Loneliness is a very painful emotion.

Many people have no clue what loneliness feels like. They blithely say things like, "Oh, I lived on my own for five years and I was never lonely." I say, lucky you to these people. They have no idea what it means, and I am happy for them.

The point is, if you have a life outside of yourself and your four walls, then you have no reason to be lonely. If those people who think they are lonely have friends, or a loving family who keeps in touch with them, they are not likely to be lonely. Just being by yourself for a few hours a day does not equal loneliness. And people nowadays have computers and cell phones where they can keep in touch with others in their lives all the time.

It is really alarming to realize how many people are lonely. Unfortunately, it happens perhaps today more than ever before as families split up and go their separate ways. People feel lonely, unloved, and think they will lose their minds if this awful feeling doesn't stop.

I think loneliness is like a bug, like a pandemic even. Millions of people the world over are suffering from this virus. It's not like you can go to the pharmacy and get a shot for loneliness like you can get a shot for the flu. Wouldn't that be nice? We could all kiss loneliness goodbye, forever.

But life is just not like that, people are lonely and that is that.

I am desperately floundering around here, because I feel as if I should be able to account for the way I cured my loneliness, but I can't really pinpoint it, or come up with a course you could follow. In fact, it would be great if you could take a course online "Cure for Loneliness,' but so far, I haven't come across a course like that.

So, what are we left with? If there is no shot and no course we can rely on, then we seem to be left to our own devices. We need to climb out of this black pit of loneliness somehow or we feel we will die.

How did I move from lonely to enjoying my own company? I keep asking myself that question. The last time I spoke to my brother in Australia, he said, "Do you ever get lonely?" I had to think for a moment, then said, "I used to, but not much anymore."

All I can say is that loneliness can be temporary, and it is possible to eventually climb out of that black pit and feel happy alone. Being alone and being lonely are two very different things, but you don't need me to tell you that. Being alone is a choice, whereas loneliness seems to be thrust upon us whether we like it or not.

If I am honest, I would say that there is no cure for loneliness that I know of. We just have to accept that that is what is happening right now and wait for it to pass.

Question 34

How do I stop feeling bitter and angry towards women? They don't give me a chance because of my mental health disability. I am having to live a lonely, miserable existence for things I can't help.

I have to empathize with you because I have been there. I remember all the anger and bitterness, and of course, the loneliness which comes with having a mental illness and not having the life that others have. It seems so unfair. And it is unfair.

Yet, that is life. Whether we like it or not we just have to accept it in the end because we are stuck with our diagnosis.

I would like to ask you if you are receiving proper treatment? That is a must if you are to feel better about yourself. It can take a long time to get it right, but when you do you will see how good it feels to be well, even if you have the misfortune to have to fight harder for what you want than others.

It is no use sitting in a corner and feeling sorry for yourself as the years will slip by all too soon without you noticing. It may be true what they say about there being a person out there for each of us. We just have to be patient until they turn up.

I would like to think you could drop the anger and bitterness because people can tell that is how you feel, and it really puts them off. You will be projecting negative vibes and nobody will want to be around you then. See if you can relax in women's company and not expect anything monumental to happen. You might be surprised. Determination goes a long way, and so does resilience. Just because you have been dealt a bad hand, doesn't mean you have to accept it for the rest of your life.

Question 35

Do older people with no children feel lonely?

I think I must come under the heading of an older person who is childless. However, whether I feel lonely because of that fact is another thing entirely.

All I can tell you is that I suffered immeasurably from not being able to have a child. It is something I feel ashamed of. I used to think it was a sign that if I wasn't a mother, I wasn't a real woman, and I hated to admit that to anybody. It was all the more painful when being around women who thought nothing about having children because it was easy to get pregnant.

I had an ectopic pregnancy when I was twenty-five while I was trying to conceive. It could have killed me. Nevertheless, my husband and I tried for another ten years after that in hopes of being successful. Nothing happened and we remained childless. It was a terrible time in my life.

You may be surprised to learn that I still have these feelings of failure to an extent, and I am now in my seventies. And even stranger, I don't think much about having grandchildren, I still feel sad about not having had a baby.

I can't say that I am lonely because I don't have children, though, as I have other things that take up my time. Seeing as I never had children, I don't know what it means to have them around.

But it wasn't always like that. The pain was so great for such a long time that I was quite incapable of looking at new babies, and my stomach was in knots if somebody wanted me to actually hold one. I was a nurse when

I was young, so inevitably, I had to hold babies during my training, but I coped by thinking it was just my job, and didn't really hurt. Although even that defense broke down one day when it became too much. I had a panic attack and had to lie down on an empty bed for half an hour. I still didn't admit that the reason I panicked was because I wasn't a mother.

It is amazing the agonies I have been though, thinking I owe everybody an answer when they innocently ask if I have children. I have struggled with a suitable answer to that question for many years. Thankfully, very few people ask me that these days. They either assume I must have had children at one time, didn't want any, or I just don't care.

People always ask me, quite sensibly, why I didn't adopt and there is a good answer to that question. I married a man (later on) who had adult children, He had also had a vasectomy. I did call an adoption agency once, but was told I was too old at thirty-nine. Shortly after that, we left England.

Now that I write this story, it seems like the end of a miserable era. I just accepted childlessness after that, and the pain subsided.

Question 36

I live with people who have a victim mentality. I have to face constant gaslighting and lack of empathy. I'm very lonely. How do I cope?

First of all, you are very astute in recognizing that the people you live with have a victim mentality. Even acknowledging that puts you way ahead of the crowd. However, the fact that you can see that in others prompts me to ask you where you are a being a victim in your own life?

It is a fact that, all too often, we see our faults in others but are unable to reconcile them in ourselves. You mention that they gaslight you and are not empathetic which, whether you care to admit it or not, is part of your victim talking to you.

That is number one, but I am still congratulating you on identifying a problem in your living arrangements. Number two is more difficult to accept. You seem to be stuck with these people who don't care about you which makes me wonder if you could take this opportunity to think about who you are gas lighting and who you have little empathy for?

People come into our lives to teach us lessons. It is pre-arranged that we meet certain people for that reason. So, this is a gift whether you realize it or not. You are being presented with a situation which you can benefit from in the future.

Once you decide what it is you need to learn about these people and the situation you find yourself in, you will be able to move on and not repeat the pattern.

Be aware, though, you will then be asked to make choices about who you live with in the future. Choose wisely. If you have truly learned the lesson of the victims who didn't care about you, you will move on to a more loving relationship in the future.

Question 37

What are the things no one tells you about living alone?

I wasn't going to answer this question because it is fairly obvious there are heaps of things nobody tells you about living alone. Some people never tell you at all.

They don't tell you how difficult it is to pay unexpected bills, how boring it is to eat on your own, and how helpless you feel when you are sick.

They don't tell you how strange your raspy voice will sound on the phone if you haven't spoken to anyone for days. It is always a surprise when you hear yourself speak.

They also forget to tell you it will be nigh impossible to administer medicine to your squirming pet when you are on your own, and when hail storms come in June, there is nobody there when the roof caves in.

They don't tell you that when the car breaks down, the washing machine leaks, or the TV needs replacing there will be enormous problems trying to fix these things on your own. It is all very well buying a new TV, but who is going to carry it home from the store, and who is going to connect it up when it gets there?

I have bipolar disorder and have often needed to go to the hospital at short notice. Severe depression, illogical mania, out-of-this-world psychosis, and suicidal plans all rendered me incapable of thinking straight, let alone advocating for myself when I was sick.

Nobody tells you what to do about your cats, the rent, the bills, the food in the fridge, or the appointments you have coming up when you have to go to the hospital at short notice. Everybody assumes that you will have somebody at home to take care of everything.

Nobody tells you any of these things, and I can't blame them. It is highly likely they have never lived alone so how would they know the pitfalls?

Luckily, I have made plans in advance for all these eventualities, but I wonder sometimes what elderly people do when they are incapable of helping themselves and there is nobody there to help them. That kind of situation can make you feel very lonely indeed.

What is the reason they don't tell you? I wonder about this, but can only assume that people who are on their own learn to accept their own company and stop hankering after a life with other people. After all, if you can't change something, you had better accept it for what it is.

When you accept something, you start to see how it can be advantageous to you. There are many plusses about living alone.

Question 38

A friend once told me that when I leave after visiting him, he is instantly lonely. Could he really feel this way or is he trying to manipulate me?

At a guess, because I don't know you or your friend, I would say that he was both, lonely and manipulative.

But seeing as you said it was only once, then I assume your friend was feeling very vulnerable the day he told you that.

Living alone is a big challenge. There is no doubt about that. You will realize that when you look at Quora in any detail and see all the hundreds of posts from people who just need somebody to talk to.

Loneliness is chronic when you have no worthwhile contacts at all. There can seem no end to it which makes it all the more difficult to cope with. This is true for many people living alone. Chronic loneliness can be very demoralizing.

But when you are acutely lonely, it is a different thing entirely. Acute loneliness comes about suddenly when the person who usually copes fine on their own is suddenly overwhelmed with problems. This could be what happened to your friend.

His problems could be with health, finances, social contacts, or many other things. There may have been many deaths in his family and he finds himself all alone in the world with no companionship and nobody to be with for comfort. Cellphones, Zoom and emails are great, but they do not take the place of a real, live person and a warm touch.

I know all about chronic loneliness because I have lived on my own now for many years. It just goes on and on. Once, when I was doing fine, I suddenly realized I had enormous problems and had no idea how to cope.

My problems are irrelevant, suffice it to say that I realized for the first time that I was much worse off than I thought I was.

I broke down and cried and was in a terrible state for quite a while. I yearned for somebody to tell all these problems to, even if they were powerless to help, A warm body in the same room would have made all the difference in the world. I might even have got a hug.

That did not happen and I felt devastated. So, I hope this will help you understand the pain of acute loneliness. Perhaps your friend was feeling the sting of that pain after you left his house. Physical or emotional pain can make you very vulnerable, and being alone only makes it worse. Maybe you could reach out to him more often and make him feel cared about.

Question 39

Do people know when they are dying and prefer to be alone?

That is a funny thing. You would think people would always want to have their loved ones with them when they take their last breath, wouldn't you?

How many times do people all gather together and take it in turns to see their loved one? And how many times do they tell them they love them and will miss them? They don't want to forget to say it.

It is a natural instinct to want to be with someone when they are dying. People rush home from far away so that they can catch the person before they die. However, it may surprise you to know that some people really do want to be alone.

When I was nursing dying patients, it never ceased to amaze me how many people just slipped away when they were alone or with me at their side. I felt it was an honor to be with someone when they died. I was glad to be with them at the end of their lives. But families get very upset when this happens, and think the person should have waited until they were there so that they could say goodbye.

Many families have been in the room a moment before, they may have been there for days, but the instant they stepped out to get a drink or go to the bathroom, their loved one took their last breath.

They were disappointed. They felt cheated. Yet, it seems to me that this is what the person really wanted. We are not privy to their thoughts, so have no idea why they want to be alone. But if that was their wish, then we should grant it.

Question 40

How does one cope with loneliness when you can't do anything about it? Everyone has their own lives and are married and have grandkids. I'm alone and sad every day and night. I wonder if it is because I am not worthy.

The only way I know how to cope with things I don't like in life is to accept my situation.

Nobody wants to be lonely, but if you are stuck with your own company day and night, you may as well accept the fact that your life is like that at the moment, and you had better make the most of it. That doesn't mean it will always be like that. It may well be a temporary situation. Things can change when you least expect it.

Ask yourself what you could do to feel loved? What would make you happy? Do you long for an arm around you, a bit of company or a nice treat?

When you find the answer, see if you can give it as a gift to yourself. Give yourself a great big hug, do things that make you happy, and grant yourself the things you would like from others. Then you will be able to forget all about the loneliness that follows you everywhere you go. You will be able to discard it like an old coat. You will be free.

Non-acceptance makes you a slave to your situation. You can never be free. Many people have tried to hang on to situations, but this never works. It is soul-destroying to keep on believing that there is something wrong with you. Being ugly and unworthy are figments of your imagination, not the truth. I am sure you are not ugly and you are as worthy as the next person.

Acceptance is key to this and most other situations in life if you are unable to change them. I hope you can find peace and love in your heart just for you. Everybody is worthy of love, and you are no exception.

Question 41

How does an elderly man adjust to the reality that he will live alone for the rest of his life?

I don't know about elderly men, and I don't know whether you will find your true love one day, but I do know it is not possible to know these things. We have to rely on fate. Or luck.

Many people end their lives living alone. It is very common indeed. In fact, 27% of older people live alone in this country. More people live alone in America than in any other country in the world. In other parts of the world, only 16% of older people live alone as the elderly generally live with their relatives in extended families, often three generations living under the same roof.

In this country we often see this kind of living arrangement in a negative light - I almost typed, 'loving arrangement' which would probably be more accurate - but that is the reason why people feel so lonely here.

The way I have dealt with this, and the loneliness, is to turn everything around and see the good side of it. I am now free to do exactly as I please, and don't have to answer to anybody.

If I feel like lying in bed in the morning, there is nobody here to start moaning and making me feel guilty for not getting up. And when I do get up, I can sit about in my nightdress, typing away on Quora or writing books, for as long as I like.

I can also go where I like, and don't have to worry about what time I get back. If I want to leave before the end of a get-together, I leave, or if I want to stay, I can do that. Nobody is here to decide on the time limit for these events. I am left to my own devices.

I could go on and on because I find that life alone is really great, but you get the point. If you can always think on the bright side, you will realize it is not so bad being alone. Never accept your own company as second best.

On the other hand, never give up hope that you might spend the last of your years with somebody nice. You have yet to meet them. Many men marry in their old age. It is not uncommon at all, and some people are much happier than they were when they were young.

We just cannot predict the future. If you remind yourself that at the present time you are free, you will see that freedom is a wonderful thing.

Question 42

How can I be optimistic? There are times when I feel happy, but most of the time I feel sad and afraid.

It may seem difficult to be optimistic in today's world when just about everything is going wrong. We live in times when, even if we are not involved, we see terrible devastation on the TV and online. There are countries at war, people starving, murders being committed, and many other things to make us sad and afraid. However, if we can manage to think positively, we shall see that we are not necessarily being directly affected by these things and life is not so bad.

The problem with allowing negativity to run your life is that you are not trying to help yourself, and as they say, nobody is going to do that for you.

Learned helplessness is when a person thinks that as everything is going to go wrong anyway, they may just as well give up. People who had pessimistic parents, bad childhood experiences, financial insecurity, or are coping under adverse conditions are more prone to learned helplessness. It is something they live with.

People who are optimistic tend to blame external factors when things go wrong. Whereas, people who are pessimistic always seem to blame themselves. However, if you realize that you can adjust your world view, you can start to think of your problems as challenges and actually enjoy overcoming them.

Optimism is a choice and the benefits of optimism are many. You can enjoy better physical and mental health, have higher motivation, lower your stress levels, and even live a longer life.

People who are optimistic believe that set backs are only temporary and they will be able to overcome them in the future. If you want to change your way of thinking, write down ten things that could possibly go wrong in your life. Then next to that list write down what you can do to change it. Be proactive, don't accept that you can't change your lot in life.

It will seem daunting at first, especially if you have never thought positively about yourself before, but you will see that, with practice, you will begin to realize that you are not hopeless and helpless at all. Once you start acting on your challenges, you will see that they are often temporary and can be overcome with a little positive action on your part. The other thing with lists like these is that you can always look back days, weeks, or maybe even months later and see how so few of these problems actually materialized.

If on the other hand, your feelings of sadness and fear are part of depression or anxiety, you would do well to see your doctor and begin treatment. Hopefully, life will change for you soon.

Question 43

After years away from home, I'm back and I can't find people who are in a similar space in their lives as me. In fact, I often get judged for not wanting what others want. Therapy helps, but life is getting lonely. Any thoughts or advice?

As they say, you can never go home again. And this is sad, but true. Home is not the same when you return. People are different than what you remember them and you find it difficult to fit in.

I am from London, but have lived in a small town in Texas for the past twenty-six years. I am not a Texan, I am not even an American, but I have to say that I have adjusted to life here after all this time. I do not hold the same beliefs as many people I meet, but even that I can learn to live with as I enjoy other things.

But if I were to go back to London, I can be sure that I would no longer fit in. I don't think the same way as Londoners think now. I remember the things I used to hold dear, but they do not matter to me now. I would find it very difficult to settle down and would not feel accepted just like you.

I can see that you are probably having difficulty with family as well. You are a product of your previous environment, not the person you used to be when they knew you. You can try to get along with family as they are, but I can appreciate how difficult it is for you.

It is true that I am not in exactly the same position as you. I am still in Texas and not in London anymore. But I know I could adjust over time if I went back just like I adjusted here when I first came. Certain situations take time to sort themselves out. You can't expect to jump back into the same position you were in before you left.

You will never be able to feel part of your environment again because you are a different person having been away for so long. You have had very different experiences than your neighbors. Try as you might, you cannot forget your last several years, and nor can you wipe away all traces of what those years have done to you. You have moved on whereas they have stayed the same.

If all seems lost at the moment, you may have to be patient and wait for other people to come into your life - people you have something in common with, perhaps people who have also left the town and come back. They are out there. You just have to find them.

Question 44

How can a lonely introvert with social anxiety make friends? Being alone is great, but being lonely is getting tiresome

You have a valid dilemma. Being lonely is soul-destroying and it can seem unending. The pain of loneliness is acute and never seems to go away.

I am an introvert and know how difficult it is to make friends. I also suffered from social anxiety for many years and know how difficult it is to try to mix with others in company. Even if you want to go out, it is so scary when you are trying to converse with other people that all you want to do is go home.

Not so long ago, I became absolutely obsessed with making friends. It was on my mind the whole time and I really upset myself. I used to spend endless hours at my therapist's office moaning that I didn't have any friends and had no idea how to make them. I joined lots of clubs and went to church but nothing seemed to work for me.

Then one day, I decided I had had enough of always searching for friends, looking at everybody I met wondering if they would be friends with me. I chose to make friends online instead. It has been a great success and I have never looked back.

I now have many friends on Quora who I write to regularly, and as some of them have become good friends, we write emails instead. In fact, one man I have become very friendly with writes to me every day, sometimes more than once a day, because he is lonely, too. I now find my online friends are more reliable and helpful than any of my friends in the 'real' world and, every time I lift the lid of my computer, I know that my friends are in there.

So, I would recommend you make online friends to keep you company when you are out of 'real' friends. It does not cost a thing; you don't need to go out to groups and you don't need to worry about social anxiety. There are many websites that have personal message boards. Find something you are interested in and you will make friends.

Question 45

How many 70-year-old women are all alone, and how do they deal with it?

I don't think anyone has done a survey of the kind you are after, but without a doubt many women in their seventies live on their own. As men often die younger than women, there are far more single women out there. In fact, it is hard to find a single man. My town is a wonderful place for retirees to settle down and it is full of widows and divorcees. Many of them are alone, but there are very few single men.

I am in my seventies and have no relatives in the same town or in the same country for that matter as all my family live on different continents in the world. But the fact is, like everything else, you get used to being on your own, and you may even grow to enjoy it. I like my own company and keep myself occupied all the time.

Everything is fine except when I need people to do the things I can't do by myself. Yesterday my microwave oven blew up and I knew that I couldn't carry it out of the house, nor could I carry in a new one. However, there is an activity center in town that helps with this kind of dilemma, so the volunteer coordinator dropped in after work and took my old microwave away with him. He is coming back next week to install the new one I ordered from Amazon.

I do understand your position as it is sometimes difficult to live alone. But if that is the situation, you will have to make the best of it. If you are resourceful, there is usually a way of managing the hard stuff. If you look around, you will soon find people who can help you when you are stuck.

The only time I miss another person is when I just want to chat about something. Nothing in particular, I just want to comment on everyday things. I would like somebody here, but that is only on a rare occasion. Most of the time, I get by very well. If I could hire a chatty person for an hour or two a week, I would. I have a very chatty friend, but don't see too much of her because she is at work.

You must deal with being alone as best you can. Make provisions before things go wrong. Be prepared and don't get caught out. I have many eventualities in place for when things might go wrong. I wear a Medic Alert bracelet in case I fall and can't get up. If I was incapacitated, I would just press the button and summon the ambulance. I have made a will and have people standing by to take care of my cat should I have to go into the hospital. I also have a list of local servicemen on the fridge so that I don't panic when I need to find a plumber or an electrician.

All these things are very important when you live alone, and you need to think ahead and make sure you are not caught out by surprise.

Question 46

What should you do when you are a widow and live alone?

It is often the case that people are alone because their spouse died. Of course, there are many other reasons why people are alone, but I would have to say the main reason is the one I have already given. It comes as a shock at first, and you wonder how on earth you are going to manage. But you will manage, given time.

Men seem to have a harder time than women when it comes to adjusting. They often don't know how to do the basic things around the house, so suffer accordingly. Nowadays, younger men are taking more of a shared position in the household which helps them in the long run. They realize their wives work, or have young children, so many men are willing to help these days which they weren't in the past.

The worst-case scenario is when one partner is totally dependent on the other. When that person dies, the partner is suddenly left to cater to their own needs and they have no idea where to begin. I have two friends who are battling on their own since their husbands died. One used to boast about her husband's cooking and say that she didn't know how to cook. Now that she is alone, she is existing on frozen dinners. Another friend, who has been suddenly left on her own, has no idea how to pay the bills that keep piling up every day.

If you are to live alone and be happy, you will need to know how to cook, have enough money to eat out, or live on frozen food like my friend. You will also need to learn how to budget your money so that you can live within your means and not get into a lot of debt. This can be a real problem if you were the extravagant partner who spent more than you had coming in. You will have to learn to live within your means. If you are left with a tidy sum in insurance, you are very lucky indeed. Otherwise, money is often a problem.

Also, there are many practical things you will need to be able to do, like change light bulbs and do simple repairs and small maintenance jobs around the house. This is especially true if your partner was the handy one who fixed things without a problem.

As for affection and sex, you just will need to adapt unless you find someone else to be with you. Many people find that companionship is the most important thing to them when they get older. You are no longer the person you once were. You are living a different life now, and it is a learning experience. You can tackle it with joy or be miserable. It is up to you.

You may well be lonely at first. This is only natural, especially if you had a long marriage or were very close. It is hard to go through these times, but you will get through them like everybody else. Perhaps you had friends before and during the marriage. That will be your mainstay at the beginning. If you can find some companionship it will help with the loneliness. You may take up a new interest or hobby, perhaps something you never had time for before. Now, you will have more time to do what you want. It can be very freeing to live on your own. Good luck.

Question 47

How can I create virtual characters in my mind to make me feel less lonely?

What a fascinating question, one I would never have thought of. However, you obviously have a good imagination so imagine this: You have trillions of characters in your mind already. They come to you in the guise of thoughts. You are you. You are not your mind, or your thoughts. What your mind thinks are thoughts coming from all manner of different things.

They are in your mind like the Chattering Monkey and bug you all day, every day. There is nobody on earth who doesn't have a Chattering Monkey in their mind, and he has a field day bombarding you with thoughts all the time.

If you want to make characters of these thoughts, you can give them names. The mean thoughts (and most of them are mean) can have names you don't like.

They tell you how stupid you are, how nobody likes you, and how you never do anything right. Those little monsters need to be taught a lesson. Why not banish them altogether and live in peace and harmony.

It will take a long time to gain this peace because your mean characters get a kick out of ruining your day, but with perseverance you can banish him and start listening to a character who has better thoughts about you. Give him a name.

This new character may say things like how generous, kind, and loving you are, and how clever you are to have done that job so well. This character is worth cultivating.

Then you can make up all different characters by the things they tell you. Make sure they are supportive of what you are doing. Invent as many as you like. Make these character welcome.

Make it fun. It is something that you will never tire of. But be sure to work on the nasty characters first and banish them from your mind. You are the predator and they are the prey, after all. You can do whatever you like with the characters in your mind. Once you have this worked out, you will never be lonely again.

Question 48

If your family doesn't support you and you don't have any friends, how do you live alone?

If the world has forsaken you, you learn to live without a lot of people. Simple as that. There is no use denying what is your reality. Many times, there is no way of changing it. You just have to accept that you are alone in the world.

It may not be what you desire, and it may seem unusual to you, but many thousands of people live alone and do very well. As they say, life is what you make it, and this is so true. If you accept that you are alone, you will make the best of the hand you have been dealt.

There is a wonderful upside to being alone. You can do exactly what you want to do. If you wake up one morning and don't feel like eating breakfast you don't have to sit down at the table and have your Cornflakes. You can have your Cornflakes for dinner, if you like. Nobody will complain.

If you want to go to a concert and have nobody to go with, go on your own. You can have a marvelous time on your own and you don't have to put up with anybody wanting you to do what they do.

Living alone is loving alone. It is the most amazing opportunity to be kind to yourself. Instead of doing, doing, doing for others, you are now free to do exactly what you like. It is a luxury that people who live with others cannot even imagine. You may have already brought up a family, so now you are free to do as you please. Be kind, love yourself, and enjoy your own company.

Question 49

I am very depressed and lonely and can't seem to get out of it. How should I cope?

I am sorry to hear that you are feeling so sick, and can empathize as I have been in your situation many times before. It is a very lonely place to be, and very tiring. It is bad enough being depressed, but when you have nobody there to help you, it is even worse. It is true that some people are not much use when it comes to coping with a depressed person, but it is nice to have somebody nearby should you need them.

The first thing to do is to see your doctor and get treatment for your depression? Once you have medication you will likely start to feel better. Remember, it takes the medication at least two weeks to take effect, and can take as long as a month.

Depression is all consuming. You have no energy and no motivation to do anything at all. You have probably run into some problems with sleeping and eating as well which makes it doubly difficult to manage your days. Perhaps you have got to the stage of thinking about death and suicide. This is so common it is actually one of the symptoms of depression. The main thing is to make sure you don't carry out any suicidal plans.

That is a permanent solution to a temporary problem.

The thing to do is be kind to yourself. Now is the opportunity to learn how to love yourself, treat yourself like you would treat your own child or a good friend. Remember to listen to your body. If it tells you that it is exhausted, be sure to stop what you are doing and rest. Make sure you get enough sleep as well. Regular sleep will make you feel much better. But, as you may know, people who are depressed often have trouble waking up as they sleep twelve to sixteen hours a day. This is called hypersomnia and is another symptom of depression, so not unusual at all. Be kind to yourself, allow yourself to sleep for long periods when you are first depressed. If it goes on too long, that is different, and you will need help. That is the time to contact your doctor.

I wish you weren't feeling so lonely, but that is not something that is easily fixed. You may not have friends or family so there is no point me telling you to get in contact with them. Perhaps you have somebody you could call, though, as you may need some company for a while.

It is very difficult trying to cope with depression when you are on your own. There is no easy answer. The best thing you can do is to keep forever hopeful that you will get out of it as quickly as possible. I hope you will feel better very soon.

Question 50

If you live alone, how do you take care of yourself if you are ill?

Being ill can be a big problem when you are on your own. This is why you need to think about this situation carefully before it actually happens in order to be prepared. Sometimes, there aren't many options, but you need to have a plan in place so that you do not panic when the time comes. And it almost certainly will come as you are more prone to illness and accidents the older you get.

I have managed to devise a plan which works for me:

The Activity Center in my town has a program called the Reassurance Program for older people living at home alone. I have to call them between eight and ten in the morning to let them know that I am okay. If they don't hear from me, they will call me after ten. If they are unable to get hold of me, they will call my friend to go and check on me. If they are unable to get hold of her, they call the police.

I often forget to call them in the morning, and have had the police on my doorstep more than once checking to see if I am okay. At one time, they came while I was in the shower and that was embarrassing, to say the least.

Many people, me included, have a Medic Alert bracelet or pendant. The Activity Center has a program where you can get a Medic Alert bracelet or pendant for $35 a month. If something goes wrong and you are unable to help yourself, all you need to do is press the button and the company will call an ambulance for you. You can buy these bracelets or pendants from many companies. They advertise in magazines, or you can enquire at any pharmacy.

I have already made arrangements for my cat to be taken care of should I be taken to the hospital for any reason. Upon admission, the hospital will ring an acquaintance and tell her that I am in the hospital. She will call the pet sitter who has already agreed to take care of my cat. If I am in the hospital for a long period of time, I have made arrangements for a local shelter to take care of her.

Another thing I have in place is a list of all the things I need to do if I should be taken away for any length of time. I keep that list on the fridge. Of course, some of these things cannot be done at all if I am really ill or badly injured, but if I am able, I grab my purse, my keys, my phone, my small address book, and the flash drive to my computer. I already have a bag packed with some spare clothes and slippers which I keep under the bed.

Whatever you decide to do, be sure you are prepared should the time come that you are rushed away from your home without warning.

Question 51

How many people experience feelings of loneliness even when they are married?

I don't know how many people experience feelings of loneliness when they are married, but it is definitely true that many people are lonely in a partnership, even if they have a family.

When some people get married, they think they are going to be made whole in some way. They think once they have met Mr. or Miss. Right, all will be well and all their fears of the future will be taken care of. You have heard of people who proudly claim that they have met their better half as if they are not a whole person in their own right.

What they fail to realize is that their partner, whether they realize it or not, has fears of the future as well making each other's experiences very painful. We are not half people, after all, so cannot expect to be whole upon marriage.

Also, we are unable to see into another person's mind, no matter how much we would like to, so we have no idea what the other person is thinking.

Other people are lonely because they have limited conversation within their marriage. Women, in particular, like to know what their husbands are thinking. And many men will say they are not thinking about any-thing which is no basis for a conversation. Of course, this problem can be the other way around, too, when women are quiet and men want to talk!

There are many other reasons for loneliness. In some cases, a person may work away from home, or if they work at home, they may be unavailable for many hours of the day. It is difficult to say what happens in any mar-riage, but it is true to say that many people do feel extremely lonely.

The only way to overcome this loneliness, is to discuss the important things that will arise in your marriage before you get wed. You will want to know whether the other person has the same religious beliefs, wants to buy a house, wants children, is able to take care of their finances and many other things beside. If you discover that you are not on each other's wavelength before marriage, it may well be time to call off the relationship. It can be very lonely when you disagree on the fundamental aspects of any partnership.

Of course, if you did not discuss these things before, you will find all kinds of uncomfortable circumstances arising.

The worst kind of loneliness is when we contemplate our partner's death. Whether we are religious, or not, this can be a very worrying topic. Nobody knows what will take place after death and this can bring up many existential fears. It is essential that you are able to discuss this subject with your partner before the time comes.

Question 52

How bad is loneliness and depression for your mental health?

Loneliness is awful no matter what, but loneliness together with depression is very bad for your mental health. In fact, just being depressed tells you that you are not healthy mentally. Depression is a mental illness, after all.

If you are truly depressed, you are likely to isolate as that is one of the symptoms of depression. You probably don't want to be around people at all and prefer to stay by yourself. It is possible that you have given up on your friends and relatives and not made it easy for them to help you. People want to help others who are depressed, but if you isolate you don't give people a chance to help you, you will likely get more depressed.

Isolation can lead to loneliness. We all need people at some point in our lives, even a friend to chat with on the phone now and then. But when you are depressed, you can't be bothered with people and unknowingly invite loneliness into your life. It is catch 22. We want to be alone when we are depressed, but when isolating, we end up being lonely.

That is a very upsetting state to be in, but not at all uncommon. It is certainly not good for your mental health. Only you can know what you can do about it. Perhaps you can make small inroads to being with people - a phone call, an email, a text. Just to break the ice and make contact with the outside world.

Being isolated is very bad for depression as you have found out. Do try to reach out if you possibly can.

Question 53

Is it a good idea for people who are feeling deep loneliness and abandonment to meet to support each other?

Support groups of all kinds are often really helpful to people and there is no reason why this kind of group couldn't help you. If you are serious about meeting with other lonely people you could possibly find a support group in your area. There may well be a successful group you could join and have an opportunity to make friends. You might also consider joining an online group where people can help one another. They usually have a private messaging system where you can get to know other people in the same position as yourself.

However, I have found that joining this kind of group does not always benefit you. It certainly didn't benefit me. I have a mental illness and used to go to a clinic every so often to meet other people. There was all manner of groups where people could interact. As it was a clinic, the meetings were usually geared towards coping with a particular life situation, and people seemed to get a lot out of these meetings.

But the problem I found was you find yourself surrounded by people who are sad and depressed. That is why they go to the group in the first place. They are very often introverted and shy, so don't necessarily have much to say and don't start up a conversation. I found it difficult to make friends at these groups and didn't like the negative vibes these people gave off.

Eventually I found these meetings too depressing, so stopped going altogether. It was a relief not to be around people with the same condition as myself. So, you may not find a group of lonely people to your liking. It would depend on your personality.

If there are too many other people all the same; i.e., lonely and abandoned, it ends up being The Lonely-Hearts Club Band, and it becomes a place for sob stories whereas you really need people who are positive in your life who can build you up, think for today, and look forward to a bright future.

Also, the idea of abandonment seems very grim to me. People who have been abandoned often have very low self-esteem and are always petrified that the next person will abandon them if they dare to get fond of them. It is difficult to make friends with people like this.

So, you might be at a disadvantage all round with people who are in the same unfortunate position as yourself.

I think it would be far more beneficial to you to go out to meet people who are happy and have optimism that is catching. You need your spirits lifted up, not pulled down by sad people.

Find something you are really interested in, then join a club. Don't rush to make friends, just take your time to get to know people. Go for the more extroverted people who are generally happy. Maybe a bit of their happiness can rub off on you.

Question 54

How do you know if you are depressed, or just lonely?

Loneliness is pretty depressing, isn't it? No two ways about it. I have been lonely a lot so know exactly how you feel. I have also been depressed many times with bipolar disorder.

Being lonely usually means having nobody - no family, friends or even acquaintances, and it can be very depressing indeed. Loneliness often happens to the elderly who are unable to get out of the house for one reason or another. They may be disabled or just too ill to leave home.

There are definite reasons for loneliness. You may feel isolated, down, dreading the future, ashamed even to be alone, and not wanting to mix with other people even if you are able. There are no medications for loneliness because it is not a recognized illness.

However, there is a big difference between loneliness and depression, and it boils down to symptoms. With loneliness there are no symptoms, as such, because loneliness is not an illness. But when you are depressed, you will have definite symptoms:

- Too much or too little sleep
- Feelings of hopelessness, guilt and sadness
- No motivation to do anything, even things once loved
- No appetite or eating too much
- Feeling exhausted all the time
- Pessimistic thoughts
- Losing interest in personal hygiene
- Constant thoughts of death and dying
- Crying for no reason

What is worse? That's hard to say unless like me you have been lonely and depressed many times. I would say loneliness was worse for me because there seems to be no end to it, and that could well be true. It is a feeling of being cut off from the rest of the world, and this can lead to shame because it appears that nobody wants to be with you. Shame is not something other people understand. They say, "Oh, you should go out, take a walk in the park, meet people."

What they do not realize is that a simple walk in the park means seeing families walking with their kids, moms pushing babies in strollers, couples on bikes, and all manner of families and friends having a good time. It is very difficult to spot someone on their own unless they are jogging or cycling through the park. Sitting down talking to the ducks is one thing, but that can get old very quickly. I find that it sometimes feels shameful if you have nobody to be with.

Whereas when you are depressed, although it is terrible, you can attribute it to an illness and think that it will get better with medication or time, or both. A depressed person may feel lonely for the time that they are ill, but they do not necessarily feel shame for being in their condition unless they identify with the depression. Shame comes from who you think you are, not guilt from what you perceive you did wrong.

If you are feeling depressed, do see your doctor and get some suitable treatment.

Question 55

How come I'm a little too comfortable with being alone? I'm not depressed, I just like my solitude.

I expect you are questioning yourself because people keep asking you how can you bear to be alone all the time? Many people need company; they feel the need to interact with others if only to pass the time of day, but there is nothing wrong with liking your own company. It is sometimes preferable to being with somebody else.

As you say, you are not depressed, and that would be the main thing to worry about. It is very true that people who are isolated have a much higher incidence of depression, and those who are depressed want to isolate so they do not want to make an effort to go out and meet people.

It seems to me that you just enjoy being alone, in solitude, as you say. I would be glad of that, if I was you, because you hear of so many lonely people out there who are desperate for somebody to talk to.

I wonder what you do to pass the time? Perhaps you have hobbies and interests that keep you occupied. It is always wise to have things to do, especially creative things as the time passes rapidly when you are in a creative mindset. People who don't think of themselves as creative often have a hard time passing their days. Yet, there are many things people can do that you wouldn't normally think of as creative. They can cook, arrange flowers, even hang pictures on the wall and make a comfort space to live in. Those things are creative in their own way.

Stay busy and enjoy your own company. Life is too short to waste it on being lonely. I am happy for you.

Question 56

How is social media impacting seniors? Are they feeling more connected or more lonely due to the fast-paced online world we live in?

I would say social media is very helpful to many seniors. It cuts down on boredom and helps with loneliness. It is now much easier to keep up with family and friends, and if you are alone this can be very helpful indeed. Many people spend a lot of time on various social media sites, but who is to say they shouldn't? If it keeps people happy and feeling connected, what is the harm in that?

Most seniors are quite capable of learning about computers. It may take them longer because they are not in school anymore, but there are numerous computer classes that help people learn all about new technology. Many older people still like a challenge, and learning new things is good for the brain.

It is fun to send pictures back and forth and to know what the grand children are doing. Sometimes, families live thousands of miles apart and would never see each other if they didn't use social media. This new way of life has a lot of advantages, and I am not sure I can find any disadvantages right now. You may think otherwise.

At one time, I had no interest in social media and thought people used it for frivolous purposes. I used to read about people going into the kitchen to make a peanut butter and jelly sandwich and decided early on that I would avoid that kind of thing. But I have rejoined Facebook quite recently, in order to promote my books, and my life has changed considerably.

I am now interacting with people in different writing and podcasting groups, learning from them, and giving advice where needed. I have an author page and keep readers up to date on the progress of my books. I find many people are cheering me on which is a new experience for me.

Six months ago, I decided to form a Facebook family group as I felt lonely and wanted to find relatives who had been missing from my life for many years. I was in touch with a brother in Australia, but that was all. I knew there were many relatives out there, I simply had to find them. Soon enough, I was in touch with a number of relatives on this family group and now have sixteen family members who read my blogs quite regularly.

I have found a niece and a nephew in England, a nephew in Switzerland, a niece in Spain, and a cousin in Turkey. Also, extended family members have got in touch with me. It has been quite remarkable, and we now correspond regularly on Facebook and often do Messenger or Zoom videos.

Question 57

What do I have to do to end the bad feelings of loneliness? I can't start conversations with people, and feel they hate me or speak to me as a curtesy. Nobody understands me.

I live alone, so have inevitably felt lonely a great deal over the years. I have always felt different from others - the outsider - and indeed I used to think there could be a ring around me separating me from other people. I felt ashamed that I was alone. Rightly or wrongly, I thought I was in my situation because nobody wanted to be with me. Like you, I thought they hated me.

Perhaps this is how you feel when mixing with others. Of course, nobody feels the same way as somebody else, but when you have many abortive attempts at socializing, it does make you feel like the odd one out as if you are lacking in some way. It is impossible for people to understand loneliness unless they have experienced it themselves. We can never understand another person's situation if we haven't lived it.

You ask me what you should do, but that I can't tell you. In order to cope with my feelings of loneliness, I used to keep myself to myself and totally ignore big gatherings. I avoided talking about my loneliness to anyone. But it has to be said that this is not fun, or an ideal way to live. It would be better to choose your company wisely and only keep in contact with people who participate in the same things as you.

If you are interested in photography, bird watching, or square dancing, for example, there will usually be a group near you where you can meet like-minded people. I joined an art group a few years ago and made a few friends there. I have kept in touch with them over the years.

One thing you have to be aware of is that people, no matter who they are, will never understand you. It is not possible. Nobody else can get inside your head and be able to tell what you are thinking. It is highly unlikely that you can understand other people, or maybe even yourself. So, I would stop worrying about being understood, if I was you.

Question 58

**My wife died six months ago and I miss her a lot.
We had a wonderful marrige and she was the love
of my life. Now I am feeling really lonely and wonder
what I can do to find someone for companionship?**

I am so sorry to hear that your wife died. You seem to have had an ideal marriage, something that is difficult to find these days. But now you are lonely, so it may well be time to meet someone else for companionship, like you say.

The problem is, you are unlikely to find someone who means as much to you as your wife, and it would be unfair to compare other women to her. Many widowed people go through this experience of being alone and not enjoying it. If you have always had a good relationship with somebody, it is likely to be very difficult to replace that. But it does mean that another good relationship may well be possible.

One thing you have going for you is that you are a man. Single men are hard to come by these days as there are far more single women out there. So, you definitely have the advantage. If you don't believe me, just go to a church or join a club and you will see that women outnumber men by about seven to one.

If you haven't tried to meet people through churches or groups, I thoroughly recommend that you give it a try. Even if you don't find the perfect someone, you will have the companionship that you desire. And you are likely to find someone you can strike up a conversation with. The best thing to do is to think about your interests and go to a club that will have a group based on those same interests. You are bound to meet a lot of interesting people then.

I wonder if you have thought about online dating. Don't be shy. It is well known that men are in short supply on these dating sites, so you would likely have your pick. Also, it is much easier to make contact with people on there because there is no rush to get to know them. You can take your time and correspond to see if you have things in common. It is an amazing fact that a third of all marriages are made through online dating groups these days.

I wish you well, whatever you decide to do.

Question 59

What is the first thing that comes to mind when you are alone?

When I am alone, which is practically all the time, I thank God I don't have anyone here to bother me. Seeing as I was married to a controlling husband for eighteen years, his words still ring I my ears:

"Where are you going?"

"When will you be back?"

"Who are you going with?"

"Where's my dinner?"

"What's taking so long?"

"Aren't you going to feed the cat?"

"Turn the heat down."

"Switch that thing off. I decide what's on TV."

Now I come and go as I please and it is bliss, pure bliss.

Of course, this may not be your experience at all, and it will make you laugh. You may also wonder why I put up with such treatment for so long, but when you are in a foreign country with nowhere to go, it is difficult to up and leave. Nowadays, my life has changed, and I don't think I would be able to live with a person like that again.

Question 60

Why do we feel lonely even when we are around people who genuinely care for us?

Feeling alone in familiar company is common, and I believe it is due to the fact that we are individual, sentient beings. There is no doubt about it, there is only one of you in the world. Even if you travel far and wide, you will never find your double, unless you are an identical twin. Even then, you would probably have a different take on life and not be like your twin at all. When you are a unique individual, you are very likely to feel alone in company on occasion. You can feel like a stranger when you don't fit in.

When people are in a group, they may seem connected to one another, but that is not necessarily so. They are all different and separate people. Often, they are so busy integrating with one another that they are not aware of themselves at all. They lose touch, if only temporarily, with who they really are. But the moment they become aware of themselves as separate from the group, they feel isolated and scared.

This is an existential phenomenon. A spiritual dilemma.

Quite subconsciously, we become aware of our existence as a separate being and question our purpose for being alive. This can be very frightening, especially if you think you have no purpose for being on this earth. This type of philosophical thinking is something many people try their best to avoid. That is often why people like to be in a crowd. They don't get time to think of these things.

People who feel alone despite the love of others are suddenly faced with the age-old questions:

"Why am I here?"

"What is my purpose in life?"

Of course, there is no definitive answer to either of these questions, although philosophers sometimes think they have found it. But because there is no answer it makes us feel very vulnerable indeed. If you take it one step further and spend more time feeling separate from the group, you might also realize that you are mortal which is possibly scarier depending on your view of life. Nobody likes to think of their demise, and many people cannot bear the thought of their own death.

In the long run, it is best to accept that you are only part of a group, you are not a clone. Just because others are family and friends, you are a separate person in your own right, and you have got to make your own way in this world.

Question 61

Can anybody share their success story of overcoming loneliness and finding happiness? I am an extremely lonely person who has nothing to look forward to.

First of all, there is no such thing as overcoming loneliness and finding happiness. These are two very different things. You may overcome loneliness, but that doesn't mean you will be happy.

The fact is, because we are human beings, we are destined to be lonely at times no matter who we are, or how many people are in our lives. And likewise, we will be happy sometimes, but not all the time. Happiness is not an end state. People have good and bad days. It is only natural.

However, I do understand your situation very well seeing as I have been lonely more times than I care to mention. Loneliness is a dreadful thing, and I wouldn't wish it on anybody.

Whenever you mention a problem with loneliness, it is natural for people – even me - to come up with a laundry list of practical solutions - go out and meet people, join a church, join a club, go to the library, go to classes, etc. but although that might be nice, sometimes this is not possible. Also, what people don't understand is that just by going out doesn't ensure you will make friends, in fact you can find yourself feeling lonelier than ever when surrounded by a lot of people who are having a good time. All these places end up being just buildings with four walls, and you are no better off than when you stayed at home.

You asked about my success story, but I don't think I can say I am never lonely, even today. But I will share with you how I have dealt with this. I am a spiritual person and work very hard on coping with this life in a spiritual way. It's really all we have. So, when I think about a problem like this, I come up with the same answer I would have to any other problem.

I just let go and accept my situation.

Sounds harsh. Yes, perhaps. But what else can you do? You can go crying and screaming but you will still be in the same situation so you might as well accept it. If you had cancer, you would have to accept it. If you had your leg amputated, you would have to accept that, too.

Once you accept your situation, you begin to own it. Then you can do something about it. In my case, I have many interests and hobbies so have taken a great deal of satisfaction out of doing these things, not as a distraction from the loneliness so much, but for the sheer joy of doing them.

I don't know your life so can't begin to think of how you could fill it, but you will know yourself. You can tackle any problem at all by following the spiritual path of acceptance.

Question 62

What can be done to reduce the loneliness experienced by seniors living alone?

It is a sad fact that when you get into your senior years, you may very well suffer from loneliness or depression at some point. Many older people are widowed or divorced and, if they don't have any family, living alone or in a nursing home is inevitable. Even if they do have family to live with, that is not to say it is a happy situation. There are many dysfunctional families in the world, and many people would prefer not to have family members living with them. Other nations respect the elderly and live in extended families. But that is not the situation in the West.

Also, many health problems contribute to loneliness. People with memory loss, deafness, heart disease, brain diseases and loss of mobility often suffer as communication with others can be very difficult. Others have poor social skills, and feel empty and unwanted. This can lead to isolation, depression and even suicide.

It is no use trying to generalize, as being lonely and depressed is unique to each person. Some people do well on their own, others do not. But avoiding loneliness and depression is not easy when you live alone.

If you find that you are getting depressed, I would say the first thing to do is to see your doctor and get treatment. Depression is a terrible thing, and it is painful to live with.

Now that we have the internet, there is no excuse for boredom, and with Quora and other social media it is easy to make friends with people who have the same interests as you. I find these people are far more interesting than most people I meet. But, by all means, join clubs and go out to meet people if that is your only option. Many people find joy in meeting people in the same situation.

Question 63

My only son has married a woman I don't approve of so we no longer speak to each other. What can I say to him to make up for the loneliness I am feeling?

I am sorry you have this dilemma and don't know what to do for the best. I am sure it makes you feel lonely when you are cut off from the only child you have. Most people who don't get on with their child's partner learn to live with it for the sake of the family and any children they might have. To be cut off like this must be very painful, and I can understand your loneliness.

If you are serious about wanting to make up with your son and his wife, you have to do some self-examination. You say you don't approve of your son's wife. That is a very bold statement. I have no idea what you don't approve of, but your disapproval is ruining a relationship that could be wonderful.

Have you ever thought deeply about why you are such a disapproving person? What is it in you that makes you think you are better than your son's wife? If you don't approve of her, it is highly likely that you don't approve of other people in your life, and even more likely that you don't approve of yourself.

You might like to contemplate where these disapproving feelings have come from. It is highly likely that they were present in your childhood. Perhaps you had a disapproving parent who taught you to disapprove of yourself. What is it that you could do to stop all these disapproving thoughts that are making you so unhappy?

You realize that you are being judge and jury when it comes to your son's wife? Your son obviously loves his wife if he has broken ties with you. He is the go-between in this relationship. This is why you should try to make it up with both of them, for your son's sake, if not your own.

What you say to him will have to be your decision, but once you put away your judge it will come to you. In order to go from judgement to acceptance, you need to examine where you are failing. Once you have done this thoroughly, you will be able to see that love is better for all of you. Good luck in your endeavor. It is always better to live in harmony with people, and it looks like you are going to have to be the peace maker if you are to cure your loneliness.

Question 64

What should I do to overcome the feelings of loneliness?

This answer could vary because it depends to a very large extent on your circumstances. If you choose to live alone, it is unlikely that you will be lonely because you will probably have family you can call or visit, neighbors and friends you can socialize with. Or you may make use of social media like Facebook or Instagram. In this instance, you are not alone at all. There is always someone you can get in touch with.

However, for a person who doesn't choose to be alone, loneliness is inevitable. There may be a thousand things you can do in a day to fill up your time, but if you are without all the people I have mentioned above, you will undoubtedly be lonely, at least on occasion.

To answer your question, I would say that you can't avoid loneliness if you have not chosen to be alone. I have lived alone, with the conditions above, for years now. Although, I have many interests and more things to do in a day than I have the time for, I do not have company. We are social beings and need to relate to others. If there are no others you will inevitably be lonely at some time.

I think we may have to accept loneliness instead of trying to avoid it all the time. It is painful, there's no doubt about that, but I think that if you accept it as part of your life, the loneliness will be lessened.

I used to have severe bipolar disorder, so had a lot of depression. I keep reading on here about 'fighting' depression and I have done that all my life. But I am now beginning to realize that fighting depression did not make me any less depressed, in fact it worsened it because it proved to me how I had failed to do all the things that people say you must do when depressed.

I have since begun to look at depression in a new way. Instead of all this fighting, I have begun accepting depression and am listening to my body's needs. So having said all that, I accept my loneliness, relax into it, and hope that it passes quickly. I hope you will do the same.

Question 65

What do you love to do when you are suddenly alone?

Instead of feeling sad that I was alone, I took a big leap of faith and opened a new, exciting chapter in my life. And so can you. I cannot know your circumstances, but can imagine you are new to being alone. I am going to assume that you are looking forward to some alone time.

This is the time to plan a life for yourself, one that will be wholly satisfying. While you were surrounded with people, I am sure you had to pay a lot of attention to them and spent your time sorting out their problems.

If you are a mother (or father) no doubt you will have spent much of your life pleasing your children and not paying attention to your needs at all. It is not until the children leave home that you realize you have ignored your needs and it can be difficult to start putting yourself first.

Now that you have earned some time alone, allow yourself to do exactly as you please. Revel in the fact that you don't have to get up at a certain time, don't have to cook what other people want, don't have to eat according to a time schedule, and can go out wherever you like, when it suits you.

After living for other people's needs, it can be hard to accept your freedom at first. You may feel guilty or even ashamed, but remember you have earned the time so enjoy it.

Now you have all this time to spare, you need to decide on the things you would like to do to keep busy. I don't know you, so can't imagine what you like to do. But now is the time to take up new interests and further your interest in things you never had time for in the past.

If you are like most people, you will quickly find that you are so busy, you wonder how on earth you got everything done when you had to work, or were with a partner.

Question 66

Do you think you can be cursed with loneliness?

Yes, you could describe loneliness as a curse, if you like. Many people think of it as such.

Nobody wants to be lonely. People who find themselves in a lonely position during their life time often ask the age-old question, "Why me?" but, of course, why not, you? You are no different from anyone else and many people suffer with loneliness at some time in their lives.

There really is nothing good to be said about loneliness because it is a negative emotion, but you can make the best of it by going out to meet new people. I know it is scary putting yourself out there when you are alone. Nobody said it was easy. But if you want to overcome your loneliness, you will need to have people in your life.

Find out what is going on in your community. Make plans to leave the house and join in with other people doing the things you like to do. I could give you a long list of the kind of thing I am talking about, but you know your town better than I do so will only have to buy the local paper to find out what events are taking place where you live.

I hope you will reach out to other people. You will likely find others who are just as lonely as you out there. They will probably be glad of your company.

Question 67

Is talking to yourself a sign of loneliness?

I wonder what you think the answer is to your question? What would you say? It sounds to me as if you have experience of this and wonder if people think you are lonely when you talk to yourself. Or perhaps people think you are crazy because people with mental illnesses do talk to themselves on occasion. Of course, we don't know what other people think of us. That will always be a mystery.

When you are lonely, there is nobody else to talk to. That is a fact. People are social beings and need communication. Being isolated and lonely is detrimental to your health. But, none-the-less, many people are lonely so end up talking to themselves. I always say, as long as you don't do it in public you are alright.

I am alone, and sometimes lonely, and started to talk to myself about six months ago. Now I do it all the time. I don't worry about it - I just accept that if I don't have anybody else to talk to, I will talk to myself or my cat. My cat has nothing much to say, but I know she is listening!

Once, many years ago, I ate a huge peach while walking down a road in France. I remember the exquisite flavor and the joy I took in feeling the sweet juices dripping down my hand. Since that time, I have never had such a peach. However, just now I ate a peach which came a close second to my French peach. When I finished it, I said to myself out loud, "Well, that was great, wasn't it?" Nobody answered, not even the cat!

Question 68

When were you so busy you didn't have time to be lonely? What was that like?

Since my husband died I have had more lonely days than I can possibly remember. But things weren't always like that.

Ours was the kind of marriage where we did everything together. He was a controlling man and never let me out of his sight. In 1989 we left England and came to the States. We bought an RV and traveled the length and breadth of the country many times. Then we went to Europe and traveled there for six months before coming back to the States.

We crawled out of the double bed in the morning and brushed shoulders in the tiny three-foot space between the bed and the toilet, walked in single file up the narrow twelve-foot-long hallway between the toilet and the kitchen, and sat down opposite each other at the built-in table and benches in the center of our home on wheels. Ziggy, our dog, took up pride of place in the captain's chair in the front.

I spent most of my time writing. I had a word processor that lived under the dining room table at night and took up most of the table in the day time. It took me all of six years to write my novel. Some days when I was sick of writing, I would retrieve all my painting gear from a storage space on the outside of the RV. Then I would set up my easel and paint to my heart's content, flicking flies that landed in the wet paint. My husband spent most of his days doing woodwork outside the RV, and managed to store an amazing supply of machinery in the under-bed storage space inside. You could hear the buzz of his electric drill most days from anywhere in the park.

Sometimes, when we were visiting a campground for the first time, we would go for a nature tour with a guide, walking together arm in arm along the trails, Ziggy on his leash. Other times, we would go together to the local stores and fill up the tiny fridge and pantry. We ate all our meals together and watched TV every day.

So, you will have some idea of how living together in such confined quarters for so long brings you very close together. It can be claustrophobic. No time for loneliness. Later my therapist in Texas would love to say that we were joined at the hip, and she was perfectly correct.

So, when he died, I was on my own for the first time in years. The days of loneliness were long. I would sit and cry, homesick for England and write long letters to my brother in Australia.

The lonely days have lessened quite a bit since then. I only experience loneliness a few days of the year. I now cope by telling myself that I am alone but not lonely. I busy myself with keeping the house clean, doing all the errands and keeping up with my interests which are many and varied. In the meantime, I do the best I can and write every day.

Question 69

How do you successfully deal with the fact that you might die alone?

I am a nurse and know for a fact that many people die alone. And, strangely enough, some seem to choose that option for their demise.

It is common for a patient's family to sit with the dying person for hours or days, then when they leave the room for maybe just a few minutes to get some food from the canteen, the person dies.

People often get very upset when this happens, but it seems the patient prefers it that way. Perhaps to spare the family the experience of seeing them actually slip away.

Yet, the family often feels cheated and angry because they wanted to be there when their loved one died. I told them that is what their loved one wanted.

It is funny how life works out. To tell you how to successfully deal with the fact that you might die alone would be pointless because nobody knows when or how they will die. It is a big secret that our maker keeps from us until the time comes.

I visited a friend only two weeks ago and her brother, who lived with her, passed through the living room and said hello. That night was to be his last. I am sure he didn't know, but my friend found him face down on the floor in the morning where he had fallen out of bed. I am sure he didn't arrange his death. It just happens, sometimes, when we least expect it. Nobody was there when he died.

Personally, I won't mind dying alone. I had better not mind because I have nobody in my life that I am likely to be with when I die. But, then again, I don't know what the future holds either and could well be with other people when my time comes.

It is not worth worrying about something that may never happen. You may well have someone around when you die. Who knows?

Question 70

What can loneliness do to a person?

Loneliness is a terrible thing - I can sincerely vouch for that. The feeling of being cut off from the rest of the world is very hard to live with. If this loneliness continues for days, weeks, maybe even months a person is very likely to suffer many long-term consequences.

Loneliness often affects old people the most because they have usually lost family members and friends. They may also suffer from ill health and be unable to leave the house. As people age, they often become feeble and don't cook nutritious food for themselves. Then they become ill and have nobody there to help them. Eating is a very social act. People have eaten together since time began. When people have to eat alone, it can be soul-destroying.

Older people often have problems with walking, so they are unable to get to the store. If they don't get food delivered, they may have to rely on other people to shop for them. If there is nobody around, they may go for days without food.

A person who is always alone will often suffer from depression which makes it even harder to have contact with the outside world. It is very easy to isolate when depressed, and isolation deepens depression, so it is a viscous circle.

People are social animals and need one another to survive. Without contact with others, a person may well suffer from anxiety, eating disorders, insomnia, memory loss and many other things which are not alleviated without help from the outside world. Three out of five people over sixty- five will fall in any one year because as you age, your muscles atrophy therefore balance is impaired. Falling can be deadly. Many older people who are hospitalized with hip fractures never return to their former living arrangements because they die from pneumonia.

That is why it is not always correct to assume a person is managing well on their own. They may do a lot better if someone was to spare half an hour of their time to keep them company, and maybe do a little job to help them out. It would also be nice if they could cook them a meal and eat it with them so that they are not alone all the time.

Question 71

Do people choose solitude because they enjoy being lonely?

Solitude and loneliness are words that are often used interchangeably, but there is an enormous difference in their meaning.

Loneliness is a negative state of being - a feeling of isolation which is sometimes imposed by others. It is possible to be surrounded by a hundred people and still experience the pain of loneliness. It is never an enjoyable experience, or one that a person chooses.

Solitude, on the other hand, is a positive state - people choose solitude for many reasons. It is a peaceful state, an opportunity for inner reflection and self-awareness. Some go on retreats to find solitude, and many religions use this state of being for spiritual advancement.

I once went on a retreat myself. It was only for a weekend, but I was all alone in a wooded area I am not familiar with. I stayed in a little log cabin where many other people had stayed before me. There was a guest book full of signatures of the people who had visited from countries all over the world. The cabin was nothing special, but it was a place to relax and be on your own.

The worst thing was there were so many insects around and actually in the cabin. When I first arrived, a whole family (and I mean a very large family) of daddy long legs came rushing down from the rafters and into my bed. I could have screamed but that wouldn't have done any good because nobody could hear me. Instead, I waved the sheet at them and watched them disappear as quickly as they had come.

That was quite an experience, but I never felt lonely, I just enjoyed my solitude.

Question 72

Nobody truly understands me, not even my family or friends. I always feel alone and have to face every problem on my own. How can I feel better?

I have found that the majority of people feel misunderstood. It seems to be human nature. Everybody thinks others should understand them when, in actual fact, they do not really understand themselves.

I wonder if you truly understand yourself? Are you familiar with your achievements and your failings? Do you try to correct your failings or just live with them? Few people can actually say they understand themselves, and it is pointless to expect them to.

Do you know what other people are thinking? Can you mind-read? If you can then you are the exception to the rule. Most people have no idea what is going on in another person's head, even if they think they know that person well. How many partners really understand each other? It is likely that they are always doing things that are unfathomable. We are all a mixed bag of conflicting ideas and opinions. One day we think one way, the next day we change our minds and think something quite different.

It is therefore unreasonable to think others should understand us, isn't it?

You also say you feel alone and don't like facing problems because of that. I know exactly what you mean because I hate that, too. It is much nicer to have someone else to talk things over with. Sometimes, two minds are better than one at solving problems.

I am alone, like you, and sometimes hate making big decisions, but the truth is that I must accept my situation. It is no use pretending that it should be otherwise. This is how my life has turned out.

Sadly, the same thing applies to you. We are always alone, even when we are surrounded by other people. We are alone with our thoughts and feelings and we cannot expect others to understand us.

Question 73

What day of the year do you hate spending alone?

I think you must be referring to birthdays, Christmas or Thanksgiving as these are considered family days, and indeed most people do celebrate them with others. That is the normal situation, but when you are alone you have to learn how to enjoy these days on your own if you are to be happy.

First you must accept that you will be alone on those days which is a tall order, especially if you have spent them with others before. Many people have family traditions surrounding these days and it is even more difficult to celebrate on your own if this is the case.

Personally, I don't mind celebrating on my own because every time someone has taken pity of me, I have ended up in family situations that are not of my choosing. I can't tell you the number of times I have celebrated other people's rituals and am always happy that I take my car with me so that I can make a quick getaway.

The last Christmas I celebrated was when I went to my friend's house for lunch. I bought an apple pie and ended up being five minutes late because I had to line up in the store. I couldn't believe they were unable to wait five more minutes for me to show up. When I got to their house, they were all busy tucking into their barbeque. What's more, I was shunned because I was late and made to suffer a meal in silence. After we had eaten, the men in the family went off to the cinema and I was left with my friend and her mother. There were no decorations, no Christmas treats, nothing else to remind us that it was a holiday, so it really didn't feel like Christmas at all. I was glad to leave.

In my youth I had always celebrated Christmas with a turkey, and my parents put up a tree and decorations. But my friend's family must have thought they were not necessary. Nobody ate my apple pie, either.

Nowadays, I am happy to be alone. At Christmas I buy a tree and decorate it myself. I hope the neighbors enjoy my lights. I have a leg of turkey all to myself and play Christmas music.

If you make up your mind you are going to be happy with your own company, you will see how easy it is to have a good time.

Question 74

How do I cope with loneliness? I have no family or friends and my only source of entertainment is tv or the internet. I really feel I am suffering. Do you have any tips?

First of all, I really empathize with you. Feeling lonely is awful, especially if there is no release from this feeling. We are social creatures, after all, and not meant to be hermits. I also live on my own, and admit that many of my days have been lonely ones in the past. It always seemed to me that other people were out there having fun while I was stuck at home with nobody. Saturdays were the worst. For some reason I used to think families were getting together round the barbeque, having drinks, and laughing among themselves. I longed for a family.

Once, when I was in France, I was invited to a wedding and never felt lonelier than sitting with forty other people laughing and joking around a long table. I couldn't follow the conversation, either.

Sometimes, even now, when I walk in the local park on my own, the weekends are when families are out having fun. Music blares from boom boxes as I pass. I also see people on bikes, walking hand in hand, children running about, mothers with strollers, and people walking their dogs. It is amazing how few people you actually see who are alone.

However, this is not at all apparent to somebody who has never been alone. People will say they know what it is like to be lonely, but they don't. If you stay at home all the time, it seems as if the walls are closing in on you. And if you go out, you see everybody in groups having fun. Being alone is often a source of embarrassment because it appears that there is something wrong with you and you have no friends. It makes you want to just hide under the covers and not get out of bed. Being isolated is one of the main symptoms of depression.

So, I do understand your problem. I can't say I have solved this problem entirely, but have come to terms with it over the years. I have spent Friday, Saturday and now Sunday on my own this weekend. I must say that I haven't been lonely, though. I have amused myself with many distractions, one being writing this book!

I would suggest a number of things to you, but you have almost certainly thought of them yourself. You may have dismissed them because they seemed out of your reach. There are churches, coffee shops, cinemas, libraries, museums, theaters, parks and many other places to go, but they are all just soulless buildings, after all.

As I've aged, it is easier because I have a succession of doctors, chiro-practors, physiotherapists and psychotherapists to visit, so at least I am making human contact. But for someone like yourself, who spends so much time indoors on your own, it can be very difficult indeed.

What I have done over the years, is to take baby steps and talk to strangers. Try speaking to the person behind you in the grocery line, or the shoe shop, or the produce market. You will find a lot of people are just as lonely as you. I have made acquaintances at the bank, the post office, the corner store, the library and many other places. It passes a minute or two.

I am very fortunate to have an activity center in the town where I can go any time I like and participate in all kinds of activities. They have a four-course lunch there, too. But that may not be available to you. I wonder if you have a newspaper listing the events taking place in your town? You might be able to join in. You may have hobbies or interests that you could do with others. I do hope you will be able to make a start somewhere, and not stay alone all the time.

Question 75

My ten-year-old cat died recently and I can't get over it. She was my companion. When will I stop feeling lonely?

I am so sorry this has happened to you and know how you feel. I had a twelve-year-old cat that died quite recently and it was a terrible experience. I can appreciate that your cat was your companion as they are so loyal and forgiving. Pets are wonderful company.

Ten years is a very long time to have a friend who meets you in the doorway when you come home. They are always happy to see you and ask for little in return. It is very sad when they die. It can be like losing a child, especially when you are alone as cats and dogs mean more to you then. It is not always easy to make friends as you age, so pets become very important to our wellbeing.

Some people have pets but don't look upon them as part of the family. They are just there and don't really fulfill a purpose. But when you live alone, pets become very important and you end up treating them like your babies.

I have to admit it took me many months to grieve my cat who died of kidney disease. I loved her more than anything and still get a pain in my heart when I think of her. I had a horrible experience at the vet's when I had to put her down and the guilt has been terrible. Of course, we do our best by our pets, but sometimes things go awry and our best is not good enough.

I do hope you can come to terms with the loss of your cat soon. Whether you get another one will depend on how you feel. I made the mistake of getting another cat almost immediately, then found I couldn't love her as much as the one that had died. It has taken me about eighteen months to get over the death of the first cat and pour my love into my present cat. I hope you think long and hard about getting another cat. I am sure I would have done differently if I had thought it out and waited a while.

Loneliness has no bounds. It can last for weeks, months or years. I cannot say when you will stop feeling lonely as we are not privy to that knowledge. I wish you all the best.

Question 76

Why do I hate being around people but also hate feeling lonely?

That is a very interesting question, one I hadn't thought of before. I am struck by how many other people feel this way. It seems there are hundreds and thousands of people living with this same dilemma, and it is difficult to find the answer to it.

In my case, I spend 90% of my time alone and love my solitude. But on occasion, I yearn for some company. Then when I have company, I get fed up with them almost immediately and want to be alone again. It is a weird situation.

In fact, if I go out to a party, or a simple gathering of friends, I always time myself with an hour and a half, then I go home. An hour and a half seems to be my limit of feeling comfortable around other people.

If someone comes to my house, it is more difficult and I am not rude enough to ask them to leave, but I am always pleased when they go and leave me alone.

I have to say that I rarely get lonely any more. In fact, the more I am alone the more I like my own company.

If it feels any better, I would definitely say you are not alone. You just need to learn to adapt and realize you need to stay in your comfort zone most of the time.

Question 77

How do you avoid depressing thoughts when you are lonely?

Unfortunately, as everyone knows, you cannot avoid thoughts of any kind, whether you are lonely, or not. If you are prone to depression, you will think depressive thoughts. People with depression think negatively about everything. It is the nature of the illness.

But it doesn't have to be like that. You can't avoid your thoughts but you can change them. It is just difficult when you are lonely to think of good things.

It is true in psychology that thoughts are followed by emotions which are followed by behavior. It is a triangle that usually applies:

Thought

Emotion

Behavior

If you have a thought, no matter what it is, you will have an emotion. When you have an emotion, it will affect your behavior.

If the negative thought that you are a stupid person pops into your head, it follows that you will feel badly about yourself. How you behave depends on your personal style of behavior, but with that negative thought, you are likely to give up trying to improve your mind. If you are already depressed, you are more likely to accept that the thought is true.

Yet, the thought is often false, and you can do something about it. These days, we are surrounded by technology. We live in the communication era and you can learn all you want to about life. You do not need to think of yourself as stupid.

Let us say that your negative thought is, I shall always be depressed, you will undoubtedly feel sad. Nobody wants to feel depressed for the rest of their life. It is bad enough being depressed for a week, let alone feeling depressed all the time.

With that thought, you feel depressed and your behavior is one of giving up. It is a pointless thought. Giving up is not an option. If you want to get well, you need to have faith that you will get better, maybe not tomorrow, but you will get better sometime soon.

I hope you can see that the thoughts you have when you are lonely can influence how you feel and what you do. With that in mind, try to change the thought right there and then. Don't allow those negative thoughts to grow in your mind and make you feel bad about yourself.

Question 78

What does solitude bring?

There are two types of solitude. One is enforced and the other is chosen. When you think of enforced solitude, you can't help thinking of solitary confinement. This has to be soul-destroying. There are no two ways about it.

You could say that some people, through no fault of their own are enforced into solitude because they have nobody to live with and nobody comes to visit them. Yet, this is not quite true because, even if you have nobody to relate to at home, you do need to mix with people for some things. Even if you are getting up in years, you still have to eat. You may be well enough to go out and buy food for yourself, so could speak to the cashier or people in line.

If you are not fit enough to go out shopping on your own, you would need to either employ someone, or get meals on wheels. Either way, you would have someone to exchange a few words with most days. Of course, if you are not the type of person to speak to strangers, you may well be lonely.

The other kind of solitude is when it is not enforced, but rather you choose to be alone. Some people are perfectly happy on their own. This way of life can be very satisfactory for them, while other people will be lonely much of the time. I think everything depends on how friendly you are as a person, and if you want to go out of your way to talk to other people.

Question 79

Are older people living alone a health risk?

I have to say that older people living alone are at a greater risk for health problems than the general public. And this is true for many reasons.

Many old people find themselves alone later in life. It is very common. Due to the death of a spouse or partner, or being divorced, or never married at all are common reasons for living alone. Some people prefer to live alone, whereas others are very lonely.

When you have children, they may be able to help, but not everybody has children, and many times children move away and are not able to visit their single parent. I have noticed a phenomenon over the years and that is many old people decide to move to be nearer to their children only to find that in a short space of time, the children move away leaving them alone. This has happened three times in my family alone. Both my brothers, and my sister, all moved to be near their children only to find that they moved away because of job prospects or for one reason or another.

One woman I knew, moved to France to be near her family, and she has ended up completely alone because her family moved back to the U.S. She does not speak the language, has no friends, and is very lonely. I feel bad for her.

Older people have many illnesses that can cause problems when living alone. They may have high blood pressure, heart disease, cancer, and diabetes, each posing their particular health risks. Also, some medicines have adverse side effects, and older people often have vertigo which can lead to falls.

In fact, one in four people over the age of sixty-five will fall at least once in a year. I have fallen eight times myself when alone and have not been able to get up. I now go to the gym three times a week so am feeling fit and healthy these days. I should think I would be able to get up on my own now if I fell. That is one reason to keep your body healthy as you age.

I also have a medic alert bracelet which is a boon for anyone living alone as I can summon 911 at any time if I am sick.

Many older people do not cook properly for themselves and have health problems as a direct result of malnutrition. They lose heart when it comes to cooking for themselves, often cannot stand at the stove for any length of time, and also have financial problems. Some old people are house-bound altogether and cannot get out to shop or do anything else at all. It is very hard relying on others to take you here and there, and many older people hate to ask.

Then, of course, being alone can cause mental health problems, as well, and some old people are ill with depression and anxiety. Others have agoraphobia and cannot leave the house at all. So, yes, I would say that you are definitely at a greater health risk as you get older.

Question 80

Why are some people happy when they are lonely, but some people are depressed?

First, let's talk about the difference between being alone and being lonely.

Being alone means you are not in the company of others by choice. Whereas being lonely is a very negative emotion which comes about when the person has nobody to be with and is suffering from lack of companionship. So, as you can see the two words mean totally different things.

Now, let's talk about your question. You will be able to see now that it is faulty, as nobody is happy when they are lonely. It is a very negative emotion, like I have said. Many people do, in fact, get depressed when they are lonely and that is not at all unusual.

It is one thing to be lonely when you are on your own, but another thing entirely when you are lonely in company. Many people say this is the very worst feeling so avoid going out to eat or going to the cinema on their own as it is too painful. For a start they think it tells others that you are alone because you have nobody to be with, which, of course, is quite true.

You cannot tell somebody to stop being lonely if they have nobody to be with. It is impossible. You can only hope they will get through the lonely phase and move on.

Fortunately, I have been able to move on through my years of loneliness. When they say, time heals, it is certainly true in my case because I hardly ever get lonely anymore. But some people never shake off the loneliness and they are very unhappy, if not depressed.

One thing I have found that is helpful is to truly experience the feelings of loneliness in order to get past them. This sounds contradictory, but as in the case of many other painful emotions, it often works. It is very hard indeed to allow yourself to feel lonely, but if you can totally immerse yourself in the pain, you are very likely to get past it.

Once, when visiting my brother in Australia, he left the house to catch a flight the day before my flight and I was suddenly left alone in a foreign country. Against all odds, I decided to lose myself in the excruciating feelings of loneliness and abandonment. I felt wretched because it was unlikely that I would see him again as we live so far apart. He and I are getting old and it is a long way to Australia.

I let the waves of negative emotion wash over me and suffered immeasurably, but was able to leave all those feelings behind when I caught my flight the next day.

Question 81

My husband never talks to me or pays me any attention. How can I get him to change?

You and I, and everybody else, are alone on our journey. We cannot expect others to follow us if they do not want to. They have their own journey and we must allow them to take it alone. We may be with each other, as in marriage, but the journey through life's lessons is not wrapped up in marriage because we must learn our lessons alone.

You will need to understand that men are wired differently. They have different priorities than women. Men love to talk about things – the new car, their tools, the boat, the latest gadget – often because they find it embarrassing to talk about emotions, whereas women love to talk about relationships. If you don't believe me, ask any therapist and they will give you this answer. In fact, far more women go to therapy because they can't get relationships to go the way they want them to go.

Men are often concerned with their careers and bringing home the money to live on. Men are often natural providers and make a point of being relied upon in the household. So, with these generalizations in mind, it is not surprising that the sexes feel alone and lonely some of the time because men and women want different things.

It is not up to you to change your husband. In fact, he will never change if he is happy the way he is. It is up to you to change yourself so that you can be happy instead of relying on him for your happiness. If you want a friend, be a friend to yourself. Spend time doing what you enjoy the most.

You can choose to be happy. Or you can choose to be miserable. It is up to you. In order to be happy, you need to take your mind off wanting to change your husband and think of things you can do to pass the time.

Never depend on anyone else for your happiness. It is not fair, and it will not happen. People are doing what they want to do, and there is nothing we can do about it.

Be productive, keep busy. You can do many things to keep yourself happy if you try. Do some decorating, gardening, make a cake, try out new recipes. There are innumerable things you can do when you have a lot of time on your hands.

Question 82

What do I do when I feel like a piece of garbage that has no redeeming qualities and will die alone because no one will care enough about me?

That is quite a statement. I can see you are in need of a great deal of love and a super big hug. But I know that is not forthcoming and nobody has hugged you in a very long time. That is how things are, and it is very sad indeed. We are all sentient beings, and we all deserve love.

I have lived alone now for a number of years and rarely get a hug from anybody. You can't very well hold up a sign in the supermarket that says, "I need a hug. Please hug me."

The reason for this dilemma is that when you don't have love, it is very tempting to think you must always get it from somebody else. Surely, somebody out there should love us for who we are? However, with this thought comes a painful knowing that love is not going to happen, and we are not going to get that needed hug unless we ask for it. So, as I see it, the only way to get some love is to give it to ourselves.

I decided this a long time ago and don't have any problem with love anymore. And if I need a hug, I wrap my arms around myself and give my body a well-needed squeeze. Funnily enough, when you learn to love yourself, your own hugs are just as satisfying as the ones other people give you. Try it and see.

This means that we must learn to love ourselves in this lifetime or we shall always be searching on the outside for this love that we crave. It is a tall order, though, as it can take a very long time to love ourselves. But the sooner we practice, the better off we shall be.

In ideal circumstances, can you think of a loving relationship that knows no bounds? When I think of this question, I immediately think of a mother and baby as that kind of love is sacred. Most mothers love their babies unconditionally and give them all the hugs they need.

Imagine you are a baby in need of a good mother's love. Now, you must learn to love yourself in the way that a baby is loved. That means having a good mother to cater to all your needs.

If you are hungry, you need to be fed. If you are cold, you need to warm yourself up, and if you are tired, you need to sleep. These are the very basic needs any baby has no matter who their mother is. And you are that little baby who needs to have a good mother to take care of them.

Now, think about what a good mother would do to love her baby no matter what. It may take a bit of imagination at first because you are not used to loving yourself, but once you have the good mother in place, you will begin to see how easy it is to love yourself and to do things that make you happy. Never scold yourself. Always be kind to yourself. Give yourself whatever you need and that includes a lot of love. In other words, cherish the baby in you.

This is what I have done. I have a good mother who lives inside me. It has taken a long time to achieve this, but it has been well worth it. I always tell myself good things and never cause myself harm. I say I am a kind, loving person, and I truly believe I am. I think that is what a good mother would say to me. I also do things that are good for me and avoid things that will upset me in any way.

Try it, and over time, you will begin to see changes in the way you treat yourself. And eventually you will feel the warmth of your love and won't need to get that big hug from anybody outside of yourself.

Good luck.

Question 83

What are some tips on how to be more approachable in public when alone?

I was rather surprised by your question because my experience has been negative like yours. When you are alone, people do not approach you at all. You must have found that out for yourself.

I can't think of one incidence when anybody has approached me and asked me to join them. It just never happened.

I once went on holiday on my own and regret it to this day. No matter what I did people did not want to befriend me even for that short time. They were together, mostly in couples, and did not want to be bothered by a single woman in her seventies.

People do not seem to be attracted to others who are alone, especially if they give off negative vibes to say that they are lonely, and it can be very lonely when you have no company at all.

The only tip I would give to you, if you want to find someone to be with, is to approach them first. This may work, or it may not. But it is worth a try. It is a sad state of affairs, but that is just the way the world works these days. Try stepping out of your comfort zone and approach other people if you do not want to be alone.

Question 84

Why is loneliness such a profound and existential feeling?

I think you are right in saying loneliness is a profound and existential feeling. At least for most people.

When you are lonely, it is easy to stop thinking you are part of anything. Instead, you start thinking you are alone in this world, no bigger than a grain of sand on the beach, or a star in the universe. Of course, it may be true and you are alone in this world. That can be a very disturbing feeling. Then it becomes easy to start questioning your reasons for being on earth if you are no greater than a grain of sand or a star. You start thinking about your purpose and if your purpose is strong enough to make you happy.

It is the same for everyone, I am sure. When lonely, we start to question everything. If we take it too far, we start to question whether we exist at all. This is when you know you have had too much of your own company and it is time to go out and meet people.

Of course, that is often easier said than done. Many people are lonely, yet incapable of mixing with others. It is fairly common. If you don't have family or a job to go to, it is easy to become bored with your own company, living in fear that this feeling of loneliness will never end.

The thing about this, and everything else related to loneliness, is that this is what is happening right now in your life. It is a fact. And when we are faced with facts, we can either change them or accept them as they are. It is up to us.

If you are unable to change the fact that you are lonely, you are left with acceptance. And if you can accept that you are alone for the duration, you will begin to see happiness. Find something to occupy your time, an interest or hobby. Something you can look forward to doing. It may take some effort on your part, but be sure to make that effort so that you can gain some happiness in life.

Question 85

Is it okay to enjoy loneliness?

That is a strange question as I have never heard of anyone who enjoys being lonely. Some people might enjoy being alone, but they cannot enjoy being lonely because loneliness often brings pain to the sufferer.

It is just the same as asking if is it okay to enjoy being sad? Sadness is another negative emotion, and cannot be changed into happiness or you would no longer be sad.

It is semantics, I know, but I do want you to realize that you are asking the impossible. Maybe you need to deliberate on whether you mean being alone or being lonely? That is the question. It is easy to enjoy being alone. I do it all the time.

But I can assure you that I don't enjoy being lonely.

Question 86

Why does hanging out with people when I'm lonely make me feel even more lonely?

I honestly don't know the answer to your dilemma. It is very common, though. Many people do in fact feel lonely when they are surrounded by other people. I have felt that way, too, at different times of my life.

I think it might be the fact that your ego is taking a bashing and nobody likes that. If people make you feel welcome in their group and make you feel part of something, this certainly bolsters your ego. It makes you feel important that other people want to know you. When this happens, it is easy to feel confident and to forget your surroundings.

But the poor little ego that is ignored can feel very sad and isolated indeed.

I have had an ego bashing many times myself. I remember going to a dance class every Wednesday evening and feeling very lonely among the group of eight people. I could see that everybody else was having fun, they each had a partner, but I was the odd one out and had to wait until some poor soul took pity on me and asked me to dance. I used to sidle over to where the little group was gathered in the break, but was unable to join in any conversation.

If this is happening to you, I would say your ego needs to be stroked and you need to stay away from the people who make you feel small and cut off. I gave up that class and was never happier.

Question 87

My husband and I are in our eighties and not in good health. Our daughter wants us to come and live near her family in Buffalo, New York, but we don't like the cold winters up there. Should we move or stay put?

Only you can make a decision like that. You have your reasons for going and also reasons why you shouldn't go. I see you are already wondering about the cold winters. If you are unsure now, I would think you would be better off where you are. I always say, if you can't decide then don't, but that is just me. At least you say you would be living near your daughter and not actually with her and her family. That sounds like a better arrangement to me. I imagine you want to be near the grandchildren which would be very nice. You would be able to see them growing up.

One thing you might consider before making any move is finding good health services where you want to live. As you say, you are not in good health which makes me think you would need to have suitable doctors and a hospital nearby. We can never tell when we will be ill, and you don't want to be stuck in the country with no way to get to the nearest hospital.

One thing I have found is that moves like this one don't always work out because the children leave. It is quite uncanny really, but many people move to where their children live, then the husband or wife is offered a better job elsewhere and they move to a different part of the country.

I think you must weigh up the pros and cons to see whether this would be a wise move. Make a list of pros on one side and cons on the other. You can already put cold weather in winter on the con side, but hopefully there are pros to balance the equation. Just be sure to take your ill health into consideration. It is no fun being ill in a place where there are poor facilities.

You might also consider what you would be leaving behind. Do you have a group of friends that you get together with on occasion? Would you miss them, or are you the kind of people who make friends easily? You might have things in your town that you would miss. Are you a member of a church, for example? Would you miss members of the congregation?

It is not to say you can't make new friends, but it becomes more difficult as you age and many people are widowed in their eighties. To be very realistic, you also have to consider what would happen if one of you were to die. I know that is not a pleasant subject at any time of life, but you are already in bad health. If you are surrounded by strangers, you might feel very lonely.

Do consider all these things before you make a big move like this. It would be terrible to leave all you are familiar with only to regret it.

Question 88

Can online friendships help with the feelings of loneliness?

I have to tell you that my life has changed ever since I made friends online. I do have some good friends near where I live, and we do things together, but I would say I am closer to my online friends, which is a strange thing, I know.

I have three online friends that I write to every day. Yes, every day. And one of them I write to at least three times a day, often much more. We discuss all manner of things, and it is like an ongoing conversation, so it is anything but dull and boring.

This particular man is a very curious person and researches everything. I really like this as it gives us lots to discuss, and many things to argue about!

I wouldn't be without my other two friends, either, and would be very sad indeed if they ever stopped writing. I also write to lots of people on social media, which is fun. Of course, they are not long letters as you can't get much into a Messenger post, but nonetheless, it is fun to keep up with people from all different countries in the world.

So, yes, I would say that it is wonderful to have online friends and you should nurture them. If you are unsure of where to start, go to the usual social media sites like Facebook and Twitter. There you can write to people quite regularly, then you will get to know them more and they will become pen friends. Or find friends on sites that interest you. There are groups of every kind on the internet.

Whatever you do, be careful not to give out very personal information, and never give money to people who ask for it online. That is definitely a no-no as it has got people into a lot of trouble in the past. If you go into online friendships carefully, getting to know them little by little over a period of time you should be safe. But always put safety first because not everybody is who they say they are. You may think you are writing to someone your age and sex, when it is in fact a young man from some foreign country. He may not have good intentions, either.

At any rate, having online friends can definitely help with feelings of loneliness. After some time, people start to care about you and your life. It is rewarding to make friends this way.

Question 89

How do you move on when your only companion has moved away? It's someone I adored and he was my only friend. I don't know anyone else where I am. The loneliness is crippling.

When someone you care about leaves your life things change, and often not for the better. It doesn't matter what the circumstances are, if they leave you behind it is awful. And, yes, it can be very lonely.

When someone moves away from your home town, that is a big change and can be very upsetting. They have moved on so they are involved in learning all about their new life, while you are left behind feeling lonely and rejected. However false this is in reality; the feelings of rejection are real. And it is awful. Nobody likes to be rejected whatever the circumstances.

Yet, this is what is happening, and has happened, and there is nothing you can do to change it.

So, what on earth can you do? First of all, you must see this change as a loss, a great big loss. Then you can grieve the loss accordingly. You don't say much about the person, but I do know they were dear to you. No matter the circumstances, if you were very fond of them it is gut-wrenching.

When you suffer with grief you go through many stages, not all at the same time, and not in the same order. But nonetheless, you will likely go through shock, denial, anger, depression and finally acceptance. Acceptance is the last stage of grief. That is when you can say you are ready to move on. It is not to say that you won't miss them, though, as they will always have a special place in your heart.

In the end, when something has actually taken place, the only thing that's left for us to do is to accept it. It is now in the past. There is nothing we can do can change the past. So, learn to accept the present and let the future take care of itself.

It may seem harsh to you, and you probably don't know where to start with acceptance, so I advise you to let the feelings of grief wash over you until you are done. Cry if you want to. Get mad. Then, and only then, will acceptance seem real to you. Grieving is hard. It takes a lot of energy. But, at the end of the day, that is what needs to happen. So do it now and let the person go.

Question 90

I am an artist and spend a lot of time alone. Just lately I have been getting lonely and think it would be nice to have a companion. How do I go about finding one?

I am also an artist and sometimes think the same things as you. Loneliness seems to hit most people at some time in their life, but more so people who live and work alone. Being creative in any endeavor is often time spent in solitude, so you are not able to make a lot of friends.

I found this works out fine most of the time. I am quite happy here painting and writing to my heart's content. In fact, I couldn't think of a more exciting, indulgent way to live, and many people would envy that. But, as you say, you can get lonely without a companion.

I don't know about you, but I would like a companion who lives in their own house, yet meets me on occasion for a meal out on the town. We might even spend a holiday together. When my husband was alive, we did a lot of traveling and spent all our time in each other's company. It was fine some of the time, but did get a bit stifling in an RV whilst traveling the country.

So, I can appreciate your feelings of loneliness, but where to find a companion is another thing. I don't know where you live or what opportunities for meeting people you have in your town. I rarely, if ever, meet anyone my age who I would like to spend time with. But you may be lucky.

I take it you have looked into churches and other places where you can make friends? Have you tried joining a club where you can meet people with a shared interest? You can find all kinds of clubs in the local paper and it is often fun to join them.

Have you tried online dating? I know there are many people who have found someone to be with, and many have married people they found online? It is a sign of the times. I think it would be a good idea to try it and see how you get on.

I must admit it didn't work out for me, but that is not to say that it couldn't work out for you. You may meet someone who lives nearby and shares your interests.

Do you have an art class you could join locally? It can be nice to meet up with people who are doing what you love the most. Funnily enough, I had an email this morning asking if I would like to do a two-week Atelier course in the local arts club. I would have jumped at the chance, but it was very expensive and I am busy writing my next book now.

Good luck with your painting.

Question 91

I feel lonely, sad, and unable to focus on any project. What should I do?

I am sorry you are feeling so bad, but what you describe are the main symptoms of depression. Did you realize that? People who have depression experience all those things and much more besides.

It is true that not everyone feels sad when they are depressed, but they often feel lonely and are usually unable to focus on any project as motivation is at an all-time low.

Here are some other symptoms you might recognize:

- Feelings of guilt or emptiness.

- Feelings of worthlessness.

- Feelings of hopelessness and helplessness.

- Crying for no reason.

- Having no appetite.

- Exhaustion.

- Feeling slowed down.

- Thinking about death and suicide.

I want to tell you to go to your doctor if you have any of these other symptoms, but I would also advise you to go to your doctor if you are just feeling bad about yourself. There may be some other medical reason for your symptoms that you are unaware of.

Unfortunately, there is no magical cure for loneliness. It takes a lot of effort on your part to mix with others and to keep in touch with them. If you are depressed, I wouldn't think you have the motivation to do any of these things.

I would start off by seeing your doctor who may well prescribe some medication for you? Then once you are feeling better you will be able to reassess your situation.

Question 92

Why does life seem so meaningless? I don't know why I am here, so what is the point of all this? What is the point of anything?

You know, I tend to think most people go through this phase of thinking at some point in their lives. It seems to be a very common complaint and I have certainly had it myself.

When you look at life, it certainly does seem pointless at times as we are all doing the exact same thing - trying to survive. Some people seem better at it than others and certainly there are some who are luckier than others. But the whole thing about being a child, going to school, going to work, getting married, having kids, retiring, then dying at the end of our lives all sounds pretty bleak when you look at it like that. Yet it is what the average life consists of. It is the rare person indeed who doesn't follow this path.

Some people like me do better on their own, but we are unusual as most people who are alone become very lonely and certainly can't see the point of existence at all.

Yet, what are we left with? The only alternative to this pointlessness is to die, and that seems pretty pointless to me. Seeing as you are here, you may as well make the best of it.

The way I cope with this futility is to write poetry. I have written reams of poetry about life - what we do every day seems so futile, and we all fear non-existence.

So, what we have to do in the end is to keep busy doing things we enjoy and hope to have a good life while we are here. It is a tall order for a lot of people, and some people just can't find any hope at all in their lives. But for the rest of us, life is just about being happy.

Question 93

How do you start loving yourself and enjoy your own company rather than feeling lost and lonely?

What you describe is not something too many people can succeed at. It is a process, and usually a very long and torturous one at that. Many, if not most people, do not know the answer to your question as not too many people actually love themselves and enjoy their own company. You could say it is a rare commodity.

The process by which you learn all these things starts off by learning to like yourself as a person and as a friend. Be a friend to yourself first. Many people hate themselves and can see no way of ever achieving this goal. Yet, in order to love yourself, you have to take the first step in learning to like yourself or you will be lost before you start.

How do you like yourself? Well, that is simple, but not easy, as the saying goes. It is simple because you are probably a likeable person, but it is not easy because we don't come with a manual on how to like ourselves when we are born. Instead, we experience many things that make us hate ourselves. It is a very sad fact of life.

So, learning to like oneself takes us back to being a small child at home with our parents. You may have to imagine this was a good experience if it wasn't so in real life. When you are able to think like a five-year-old child you will be half way there.

What do five-year-old's do to make friends? They don't usually have a problem because they think they are naturally a good, friendly type of person. They go up and talk to someone their age and ask them to play a game with them. And, before you know it, they are bosom buddies.

Well, it is just like being five all over again, but not seeking out others to be friends with. Just be kind to yourself. Ask yourself what you would like to do, or what you would like to learn, then do that. Once you start being a good friend to yourself, you will naturally like yourself better.

Loving yourself has to go one step further and it is a step that a lot of people are not prepared to take. It involves going back to when you were pre-verbal, when you relied on your caretaker for all your basic needs. Those needs are for food, shelter, clothes and love. These are the things you will need to give yourself if you want to learn to love yourself. It can be a very slow process, or you may be able to jump right in and love yourself right away.

Ask yourself what a baby needs in order to survive? You will find they need a caretaker of some kind as they are not yet able to care of themselves and are, in fact, very vulnerable indeed. So, this means that you will need to be your own caretaker who will take care of all your basic needs.

On a practical level this might mean feeding yourself with nutritious food if you are not eating a good diet at the moment, and providing yourself with good shelter in the form of a comfortable place to live. If this is not possible, then even a tiny space where you can feel safe is all that is required.

Now you have to learn to love yourself which is the hardest thing of all. Learn to listen to what you need and supply it for yourself. This is not things you want, like a new car, or gadgets, this is things like peace and quiet, touch, and praise for things you do. In other words, you need to care about yourself.

When you have achieved this, you will have learned how to love yourself and will be happy in your own company. You will be able to pat yourself on your back and congratulate yourself for all the work you have done.

Question 94

How do you tackle loneliness in marriage?

That is a very difficult situation to find yourself in, yet so common. Many people complain that they are lonely in their marriage and, if I look back, I can identify with this because I have also felt lonely in my marriages and it has caused me a lot of depression.

But at the end of the day there are only three choices.

You can either communicate your loneliness with your spouse, separate, or let things carry on the way they are. Either way, it is a difficult choice to make.

How do you communicate with a partner when communication has broken down? And it probably broke down so long ago that it doesn't seem possible to go back to the way you were when you first married. It is difficult, and some may find it impossible altogether. But for others, you need to learn how to tell your partner how you are feeling and try to get them to talk about it. Chances are they are just as lonely in the marriage as you are.

Another option is to leave and get a divorce. Nobody likes getting divorced, but if you are unhappy in the marriage, that is often the thing to do. I have had two divorces for much the same reasons and it wasn't easy, but I am glad I did it because I ended up being able to communicate with my third husband. That marriage didn't end well, but that is another matter. At least we were able to talk to one another.

The third option is to let things jog along as before. This is the easiest option, of course, but the most unsatisfactory one as you will never progress in your situation. It will remain the same, and you will be full of resentment towards your partner.

Being proactive means stepping out of your comfort zone and that is never easy. We all like to take it easy and do the same things even when they are painful because taking a chance on another outcome is scary. You do not know how the other person will react for a start. They may get angry, even violent, or they may just ignore you and your needs which could be worse.

At any rate, you have three choices, so you may as well think carefully as to whether you want the situation to chug along unchanged or if you want to act accordingly. Of course, you may have children which could really influence the situation. I cannot know that for sure by your question. Personally, I preferred to call it a day, but that is me. You will have to make your own choice and that is not easy.

Question 95

At what age did you start to live alone and how did that go?

I started to live alone when my husband died suddenly twenty-two years ago. I was fifty-four at the time. In fact, I was the same age as when my mother died and I remember being surprised that I had actually outlived her, but of course that is neither here nor there.

You ask how did that go, and I would have to tell you that it went very badly indeed for many years. I found it very difficult to adjust. The reason being, I had been in a mental hospital coping with bipolar disorder for the month prior to his death and he killed himself on the day I came out of the hospital.

I was still ill at the time, couldn't work, and was left with all his debts. It was a very difficult time indeed. And I have to say, I was very lonely for a long time afterwards. It is one thing to live alone by choice, but when it is thrust upon you, and in a drastic manner, loneliness is bound to ensue.

I did not fare well with my loneliness, either, and became ill time and time again. This was very disheartening and I thought I would never be able to get used to my own company. But it is amazing how time really does help. Over time, you get used to your likes and dislikes and learn to be happy with yourself. That dreadful wound can finally heal, if you let it.

Now, I would not want to live with anybody again. Funny how life is. You have to accept your lot in the end.

Question 96

What is the point of having a social life if you always feel alone?

This is a dilemma for a lot of people. It would seem that having a social life is the way to go, yet if you find yourself feeling lonely in other people's company, what is the point?

I have felt this way quite often, especially when surrounded by a lot of other people I don't know. I have been asked to join friends on holidays like Christmas and Thanksgiving, and each and every time I have regretted going. I know that sounds extreme, but I am really a loner and don't mix well with a lot of other people. I can get on better with one on one.

So, I can truly understand how you are feeling. I sometimes wonder myself if it is worth making all the effort. Yet, not everybody is a loner like me, and I take it you need the company or you wouldn't be joining people socially. That is different, and I can see how this would be very hard for you.

Perhaps you feel that you don't fit in and that is a terrible feeling. No matter how well you know people, you still feel like a stranger in their midst. Sometimes you must feel it is not worth making the effort to fit in. If you are always going to feel lonely, then why bother?

I have to say, I really don't know the answer to this question as I haven't fathomed it out for myself. If you go out and mix with others you feel lonely, and if you stay in on your own you feel even lonelier. It is painful.

Personally, I have given up on meeting with a lot of people. I don't usually go to big gatherings because I know I shall want to come home as soon as I arrive. I do go out with people for lunch, though, but that is different. It is usually with just one friend. Perhaps you have people in your life that you can share a meal with or even a cup of coffee. I find it is fine to be with just one person, especially if you have things in common.

In actual fact, I went out with a friend only this week and had a good time. I am anti-social to the extent that I usually don't want to go out, but when I get there, I enjoy it. An acquaintance and I make a date to meet for lunch every couple of months just to catch up with our respective news. We haven't become bosom buddies, but that seems to suit us both just fine. We have a meal together and sit in the sunshine if the restaurant has an outdoor dining area.

I do have one friend who I see quite often, but funnily enough, we hardly ever go out socially together. Instead, we spend quite a bit of time in each other's houses. This is enough of a social life for me. I hope you can find a friend, or even an acquaintance, to share a meal with. That might be the way to go.

When you get older it is usually a succession of doctors and therapists. One woman told me once that doctors are her social life, but I think that is a bit extreme. I do hope you will find someone in your life you can be with and not feel so alone.

Question 97

I have finally had to give up my career due to poor health and old age. What can I do to pass the time?

I am glad you can see past the pain of having to give up your career. That could have been a real obstacle for you. Some people have a hard time retiring. It seems like a totally alien way of life if you have had a career you enjoyed. Suddenly, there is all the time in the world with nothing to do. In fact, the days can drag by if your life is empty.

The worst of it is that many people have been so busy working that they haven't had time to plan for retirement. Weekends may have been busy with shopping and housework, or catching up with paperwork that has been put off during the week. Suddenly, Saturday and Sunday are history and you are back at work on Monday morning. That is the way of things. That is how most people live their lives.

But now you can see that it is not good to be without hobbies or interests as there is nothing waiting for you on the other side of retirement. If you had a hobby or an interest that you hadn't had time for until now, you would have the time to pursue it.

If you are a home body there is plenty to do. You can do gardening, knitting, croquet, crossword puzzles, painting, drawing, playing an instrument, learning a language, listening to music, cooking, baking, flower arranging, social media, learning new things on the computer.

If you are an outdoor person you might like to attend local events, join local community associations, square dance, play dominos or cards with others, join painting groups, bird watching, walking, sports of all kinds, and keeping up with friends.

I do hope you will be able to find something you enjoy. In this technological era, we have so many things at our fingertips there is no excuse for being bored.

Question 98

I have been alone for two years now. Should I get a pet to help with my loneliness?

I am sorry you are so lonely, but think you are on to the right track when you are thinking of getting a pet. Personally, I couldn't live without a pet because they are such good company when you are alone. I have always had dogs and cats, suffered their loss, but got more pets down the road.

I wonder if you have had pets before? Most people have had at least one animal in the past. If you have had a pet before, you will know what is involved, and that should give you a good idea as to the amount of care they need. It is not enough to just want them to cure your loneliness, you need to be active in their care as well. This can involve quite a lot of things, so it is best to carefully consider what is involved before making up your mind. You must also bear cost in mind as it costs a lot to feed an animal, let alone take them to the vet.

Another thing you might like to think about is the age of the pet you are thinking of getting. Many people get older pets because they don't want the pet to outlive them and have nowhere to go and nobody to take care of them. This is a personal decision, of course, but I think it is one worth considering.

If you are thinking of getting a dog, be aware that you will need to walk them every day. I have not been able to have a dog because I have had so many problems with walking in recent years.

You might like another type of animal such as a bird or fish. I have no experience with this type of pet so you would need to talk to someone who is able to assist you.

One thing I would like to say is do go to a local shelter if you want to get a cat or a dog. There are so many animals doomed to die if nobody adopts them, so I wouldn't advise you to buy animals from breeders.

I have to admit, I haven't fared at all well when my pets have died. It has been a long, rough road when grieving. However, I haven't let that stop me from getting another animal. If you live alone, you need company sometimes.

Good luck with your pet or pets. I think you will be very happy to have a nice warm body to cuddle up to.

Question 99

As a formerly married person, what do you miss the most now that you're alone?

This, of course, can mean different things to different people. If you have had a long marriage, you are likely to miss the person more because they have been your partner for a long time. But if that marriage was not a good one, then you might not miss them at all.

As for me, I had a good marriage to start with. We spent probably fifteen years living quite harmoniously in England. The reason may have been that I was out at work nursing every day while my husband took care of our bed and breakfast. We were both busy with other people so had a lot to talk about on our time off. Of course, there is little time off in a bed and breakfast!

However, we jogged along pretty well for a long time, then we sold our home and moved to the United States. The idea was to travel for a while then make other plans. We ended up buying a nice new motorhome and traveling all over the country for the next six years.

You have to realize that if you are with someone day in and day out, confined to a tiny living space, things can go drastically wrong. At first it is a novelty, and I have to say we had a great time traveling from here to there, but soon enough the space seems to be getting smaller and smaller and you are rubbing shoulders whenever you want to pass by in the tiny galley.

We spent a lot of time working in various campgrounds to pay our way, and this was very good for us, but we still spent most days and nights alone with each other. Sometimes we met up with other people in the campground, and even went to cook outs where people sang and played musical instruments. That was great fun.

After touring the States for six years, we decided to go abroad and toured round Europe for six months. By this time, we were like vagabonds with nowhere to call our own. We went from place to place, met some great people, but started arguing non-stop. Sometimes, it was awful and I just wanted to go back home to England. But overall, we did get along and had a great deal to talk about.

So, when he died, I found that I was suddenly alone with nobody to talk to. I think it is the little things you comment on that you miss the most. Of course, I have got used to it over the years, but it did take me a very long time. I miss having a meal with someone and cooking for them. Eating alone is not much fun. I can find people to be with now but it is not the same as being with the one you married.

Question 100

I was very lonely but have met a nice woman who is quite a bit younger than me. I have two children who don't like her. Should I marry her?

Well, that is a dilemma. I am sure you want your children to give you their blessings, and to start off a marriage with bad feelings in your family might be very awkward. On the other hand, you want to be happy, so you must consider how much you love this woman and how much you want to be with her.

I wonder how old you are. And how much younger this woman is than you. If she is twenty years younger than you, you would need to find your motive for wanting to marry her.

It is nice for an older man to have a young woman on his arm, but as you age, she will still be a young woman. This can be very awkward in a relationship.

Do you want someone for companionship, or are you looking for a nurse in your old age? These things are very important and you would do well to consider them and even talk to your new lady friend about. She may not want the things you want and may have other ideas about taking care of you should you get sick in your old age.

Marriage to a younger partner can work, of course, but you would be advised to listen to your children and ask them what they don't like about this young woman. Sometimes there are things we don't notice when we are in love and these can be very important for a happy union.

Are you a wealthy man? This younger woman may be very genuine, but it would be a good idea to consider your will should you die first. Have you already made provisions for your children? Perhaps they are wary that this woman will get everything in your will. You will need to discuss this with them to get their viewpoint. You might like to get a prenup to be safe.

Or perhaps, instead of marriage, why not think about having a companion you can be with when you want company. It can be very nice to keep your lives separate, but meet up when you feel like going out for a meal, or seeing a show at the cinema. Whatever you decide, I would advise you not to rush into it. Regrets can be bitter. It is best to be sure you are making the right move. I wish you luck.

Question 101

I have been ill for some time and feel I have reached the end of my life. I have nobody to talk to where I live and am very lonely. What can I do?

First of all, I am very sorry you have been ill and are feeling so bad. I can well imagine what a sad time of life this is for you. At the end of our lives, we hope to feel happy for having completed a journey, but that is not possible for a lot of people, especially if you haven't been well, you are probably depleted and feeling hopeless.

I don't know the details of your life, or if you have any family. You say you have nobody where you live, but maybe this means you have relatives in other States? If so, are you in touch with them? Of course, not everybody has relatives, and sometimes when you get older there is nobody left. I know how lonely that can feel as I have nobody living near me either.

I wonder if you have people you could have a video chat with? That is a great way of connecting. Or even write to people on Facebook or another social media platform. You have probably already thought of this, though, so will not need me to remind you.

At the end of our lives, it is a time for reflection on all the years that have passed. We think of the relationships that have given us joy, and all the places we have traveled. You can reflect on the choices you have made and the lessons you have learned on your life's journey. I believe we are all here to learn spiritual lessons and this can give you a sense of accomplishment to dwell on the lessons you have learned along the way. You can also spend time thinking about the people you need to forgive and any grudges you might still be bearing. It is time to let go of all that. Time to be free.

Do you have photo albums you can look at? Sometimes, that can stir up good memories of when you were happy with other people and with places you visited. I am sure you have had some good times in your life. You could think about the connections you have had throughout your life. If you are a spiritual kind of person, you can dwell on these connections as well.

This may be a good time to think about loving yourself and forgiving yourself for all the poor choices you have made in your life. We have all made those choices. We come to a crossroad and take the wrong path. But even if you took the wrong path, think of all the people you have met that you wouldn't have met if you had stayed where you were. It is quite uncanny how our lives turn out.

You will no doubt have regrets about the people you may have harmed along the way. We all have regrets at some time in our lives but it is now time to forgive yourself for your past mistakes. Be kind to yourself. Be at peace.

To my readers:

Thank you for reading this book. It has been a pleasure writing it for you.

Loneliness is a terrible thing to experience, so maybe it has been of help to know that so many other people are in the same situation as you. At least you now know of some better ways to cope with your loneliness, and I do hope you will follow through. Unfortunately, nobody can really understand your situation as we are all unique. We all experience loneliness in different ways. Perhaps now, after reading this book, you will see a way to contentment.

At the end of the day, the most important thing is acceptance. We often find ourselves in situations that are hard to live with, but we have to accept that this is our new normal. I hope this book has given you some hope for the future.

If you have any questions or wish to discuss your personal situation with me, please do not hesitate to send me an email at:

mandala913@omniglobal.net.

I would be very pleased if you would leave me a review or a rating on AMAZON. Thank you very much for your support.

Sally Alter

Author of:

"How to Live with Bipolar"

"Bipolar 1 Disorder Rescue Plan: A Practical Guide for You and Your Family"

"A Practical Guide to Overcoming LONELINESS"

"We Never Did Mornings" (poetry)

Author bio:

Sally Alter knows the impact of mental health on our physical wellbeing. As an RN who's no stranger to loneliness herself, she thinks that everyone can benefit from guides designed to help people through the tougher times in life. With a goal of writing informative, helpful books, she also strives to be a comforting voice for anyone, regardless of what they're facing. The applicable, practical advice in her books helps readers face the more difficult aspects of living.

Sally was born in England, but currently resides in Texas. She plans to put her RN knowledge to good use in her books. She's written two books on bipolar disorder – "How to Live with Bipolar" and "Bipolar 1 Disorder Rescue Plan" - and also published "A Practical Guide to Overcoming LONELINESS" in August 2022. She is currently working on a collection of poetry scheduled for release in September 2022.

Her credentials include: being the past editor of Illuminations—Schreiner University's International e-journal. Her poetry has been widely published in Illuminations, The Muse, The Texas Poetry Calendar, Houston Poetry Anthology, Austin International Poetry Anthology, The Kerrville Daily Times and The Hill Country Community Journal.

You deserve happiness—let's get you on track!

Website: sallyalter.com

Facebook author page: SALLY ALTER

Email address: mandala913@omniglobal.net